TH[ ]

MO[ ]RN
SCIENCE

THEOLOGY

— AND —

MODERN SCIENCE

QUEST FOR COHERENCE

James A. Wiseman

CONTINUUM
New York • London

2002

The Continuum International Publishing Group Inc
370 Lexington Avenue, New York, NY 10017

The Continuum International Publishing Group Ltd
The Tower Building, 11 York Road, London SE1 7NX

Printed in the United States of America

Library of Congress Cataloging-in-Publication Data

Wiseman, James A., 1942–
    Theology and modern science: quest for coherence / James A. Wiseman.
      p. cm.
    Includes bibliographical references and index.
    ISBN 0-8264-1382-X (hb) – ISBN 0-8264-1381-1 (pbk.)
    1. Theology, Doctrinal. 2. Religion and science. I. Title.

BT75.3 .W57 2002
291.2 – dc21

                        2001053657

*To my science-and-theology students
at The Catholic University of America
and at Yale*

Contents

Preface

A T ITS BEST, theology has never been practiced in an intellectual vacuum. For many centuries, its principal dialogue partner in the Christian West was philosophy, especially in its Platonic or Aristotelian modes. In more recent times, theologians have also grappled with issues arising from the social and natural sciences, not only because of the intrinsically fascinating nature of these topics but also for the practical (and troubling) reason that real or apparent discrepancies between scientific findings and the traditional tenets of Christian faith have led many persons to abandon the latter. Ian Barbour, perhaps the best-known pioneer in the emerging field of science and religion over the past four decades, has observed that whereas for many centuries Christianity provided a total way of life for most inhabitants of the West, "since the Enlightenment, the Christian story has had diminishing effectiveness for many people, partly because it has seemed inconsistent with the understanding of the world in modern science."[1] In view of this situation, Barbour has made it his lifelong task to present an interpretation of Christianity that is responsive both to biblical faith and to contemporary science. A still better known Christian thinker, Pope John Paul II, has likewise been very intent on promoting mutual understanding between theologians and scientists, both by his acknowledgement of the serious errors of earlier theologians in their condemnation of Galileo and by his call for theology "to be in vital interchange today with science just as it always has been with philosophy and other forms of learning."[2] I intend the present work to be a significant contribution to this interchange.

Because of the vast number of scientific findings that have implications for theology, it is impossible to treat even the majority of them in a single book. One could, however, reasonably claim that the most fundamental issue is that of divine action in the world, whether that be in the doctrinal context of creation, providence, theological anthropology, or eschatology. For this reason, I have ordered the chapters of this book in the following way:

The opening chapter offers some pertinent historical background, looking at how preeminent scientists and theologians of the past four centuries have dealt with major questions arising from the findings of the natural sciences. The four following chapters consider matters that have arisen relative to the most basic periods in the history of the universe, with special reference to the topic of how we can best understand God's action within the spatio-temporal realm at any of these periods. Thus, chapter two looks at "the beginning": What does modern science have to say about the beginning of the universe and what implications, if any, does this have for the doctrine of creation? The third chapter then considers the vast stretch of time from the beginning to the present, asking what mainstream science is telling us about the evolution of entities across these eons and what, if anything, this has to say about the doctrine of divine providence. Chapter four remains within this same period of time but focuses specifically on more recent millennia, since the emergence of *Homo sapiens*, and addresses the question of what, if anything, evolutionary theory might contribute to an understanding of a spiritual dimension within humans and other living beings. The next chapter, the fifth, moves from the present to the future, even the far-distant future, and asks what contemporary science predicts about the long-term future of our planet, the solar system, and the universe as a whole and what effect, if any, these predictions might have on the traditional Judeo-Christian hope for "a new heaven and a new earth."

Building upon all these reflections, chapter six looks more directly at the underlying question of how theology can best understand the traditional teaching that God is active in the world in the light of scientific assumptions about a strict causal nexus in the space-time continuum. Finally, and growing out of my conviction that a valid theology must be consonant and coherent with scientific findings, even though it cannot simply be derived from or conflated with them, the seventh and last chapter is my attempt to demonstrate such coherence with regard to a few fundamental topics about God, human beings, the rest of creation, and their various interrelationships. Even more than the previous six chapters, the seventh explains my choice of a subtitle for this work: "Quest for Coherence."

From the preceding paragraphs, it should be obvious that I am writing primarily as a Christian theologian, and in the body of this work it will soon be just as obvious that a number of my specific concerns are rooted most immediately in the Roman Catholic tradition to which I belong. However, I have intentionally written in a broadly ecumenical way, meaning that I offer these reflections not only to Christians of all denominations but also to members of other theistic traditions and, indeed, to anyone interested in the theoretical and practical ramifications of the burgeoning dialogue between theology and the natural sciences. I am well aware that there are many areas within this dialogue with which I have not dealt, such as the very important bioethical issues arising in the rapidly developing field of genetics. I am likewise very conscious of the fact that I am not a practicing scientist, a fact that provokes in me a holy envy of scientist-theologians like Arthur Peacocke and John Polkinghorne. I do, however, believe that I have written in a scientifically and theologically responsible way and that I have even offered a number of original insights and suggestions in the more constructive sections of this work. I hope that these will be challenging and thought-provoking to my readers.

In conclusion, I would like to express my appreciation for the assistance given me in one way or another by the following persons, all of whom work in my own city of Washington, D.C.: John Golin, chair of the biology department at The Catholic University of America; James Miller, senior program associate for the Program of Dialogue on Science, Ethics and Religion at the American Association for the Advancement of Science; Herbert Wood, former chair of the science department at the St. Anselm's Abbey School; and my Benedictine confreres John Farrelly and Joseph Jensen.

I

Historical Background

T HE FINAL DECADES of the twentieth century and the opening years of the twenty-first have seen a number of spirited debates within the field of science and religion. For example, on the question of design, writers like Michael Behe and Philip Johnson have argued vigorously that the unprejudiced study of scientific data in disciplines as diverse as biology and cosmology reveals some sort of intelligent design behind the phenomena studied by scientists.[1] Although such scholars do not regularly take the further step of claiming that this demonstrates the existence of the God worshipped in the Judeo-Christian and other monotheistic religious traditions, some of their opponents charge them with allowing their religious beliefs to unduly influence their scientific claims. This does not mean, however, that all of those on the other side of the issue are without religious convictions of their own. For example, two prominent critics of the argument for design — Kenneth Miller and John Haught — are practicing Roman Catholics.[2] There is no reason to expect that this debate will dissipate anytime soon. So, too, as regards debates about such topics as miracles, eschatology, the nature of the human person, and the very concept of God and God's action in the world. The major purpose of this brief first chapter of the present study is to examine a few of the ways in which some major religious and/or scientific figures have dealt with these kinds of questions since the rise of modern science in the seventeenth century. These figures include the scientists Robert Boyle and Isaac Newton, both of whom also wrote serious works of theology; Friedrich Schleiermacher, the father of liberal Protestant theology; Karl Barth, whose critique of Schleiermacher and his followers ushered in the movement of neo-orthodoxy; and two Roman Catholic thinkers of the twentieth century who have had great influence even outside their own denomination: Pierre Teilhard de Chardin and Karl Rahner. While this examination will necessarily be far from exhaustive, it will set the stage for the succeeding chapters by noting some of the principal options that past centuries have bequeathed to theologians and religious thinkers who are active today.

God and Providence in the Seventeenth Century

It is, of course, impossible to give a precise date for the beginning of what is wont to be called "modern science." That quintessential Renaissance man Leonardo da Vinci (1452–1519) is known not only for his artistic achievements but also for his work as a scientific explorer of the natural world and as an innovator in technology. Nevertheless, his understanding of the world as a living organism was not shared by leading scientists a century after his death; for this reason, he would more properly be considered premodern. Leonardo wrote, for example: "We can say that the earth has a vegetative soul, and that its flesh is the land, its bones are the structure of the rocks... its blood is the pools of water... its breathing and its pulse are the ebb and flow of the sea."[3] Such language was soon to give way to a mechanistic one. Of the numerous seventeenth-century comparisons of the workings of the world to those of a clock, the following passage from Johannes Kepler (1571–1630) is representative: "I am much occupied with the investigation of the physical causes. My aim in this is to show that the Celestial machine is to be likened not to a divine organism but rather to clockwork.... Moreover I show how this physical conception is to be presented through calculation and geometry."[4] Significantly, scientists like Kepler, Boyle, and Newton were not only religious but were also convinced that their presentations of the world as a mechanism fostered a sense of God's wisdom and providence. Indeed, many such scientists, writing long before the academic specialization that characterizes our own era, devoted much time and effort to religious treatises. For this reason, while many of the writers treated in this chapter were primarily theologians, others have come to be known just as much, if not more, for their scientific work.

A primary reason why early modern scientists turned to a mechanical, atomistic model of the universe is illustrated by the success of Galileo's last major work, *Discourses concerning Two New Sciences*. His findings about the acceleration of falling objects and other physical phenomena were based, in the words of the distinguished historian of science John Hedley Brooke, on the ability "to relate the real world to an idealized mathematical model" and on the recognition that the process of abstraction required to do this "came more easily in a mechanical than an organismic universe," specifically one in which the most fundamental elements of nature were "precisely those amenable to mathematical analysis: the shape, arrangement, and motion of particles."[5] Galileo's contemporary, Francis Bacon, argued that such a view of the universe was much more conducive to a doctrine of divine providence than the view of Aristotelian philosophy, which at that time was in the ascendant in many European universities. In Bacon's words, "it is a thousand times more credible that four mutable elements and one immutable fifth essence, duly and eternally placed, need no God, than that an army of infinite small portions of seeds unplaced should have produced this order and beauty without a divine marshal."[6]

In the immediately following generations, many of Bacon's fellow countrymen took up the argument that the supremely ordered, mechanistic world of nature that engaged them in their scientific work was simultaneously clear evidence of a providential God. The English scientist who arguably best represents the way in which religious implications were drawn out of this mechanistic view was "the father of chemistry," Robert Boyle (1627–91). Although he is best known today for his work on gases and the corpuscular theory of matter, Boyle also wrote numerous theological treatises, many of which were published in a three-volume edition several decades after his death.[7] Like Kepler, but even more frequently, Boyle reverted to the imagery of a clock to exemplify his conception of the natural world. In particular, he often cited the complex clock of the Strasbourg cathedral as something that was in itself lifeless and unconscious and yet clearly the result not of chance but of skilled workmanship. So too, he argued, the universe as a whole is a fine mechanism whose well-ordered working reveals a divine Artificer:

> And as it more recommends the skill of an engineer to contrive an elaborate machine so that there should need nothing to reach his ends in it but the contrivance of parts devoid of understanding, ... so it more sets off the wisdom of God in the fabric of the universe that He can make so vast a machine perform all those many things, which He designed it should, by the mere contrivance of brute matter managed by certain laws of local motion.[8]

Boyle could thus use mechanistic, clocklike imagery to argue for the *general* providence of God as the benevolent source of the universe as a whole and for our need to adore such a Being, this being the main theme of his treatise *Of the High Veneration Man's Intellect Owes to God* (1685). However, he simultaneously ran up against the difficulty of reconciling this clockwork mechanism with the doctrine of *particular* providence as this had traditionally been illustrated through Christian teaching about the reality of miracles and the efficacy of prayer. To be sure, Boyle did not deny that miracles had occurred, above all in the early church, but as he grew older he moved more and more away from any emphasis on particular providence. In *A Free Inquiry into the Vulgarly Received Notion of Nature* (1686), he wrote that "it much more tends to the illustration of God's wisdom to have so framed things at first that there can seldom or never need be any extraordinary interposition of His power."[9]

This development in Boyle's thinking was mirrored in that of many of his scientific contemporaries, who in England were often known as virtuosi. It was not yet so evident in the thought of his slightly older colleague Dr. Walter Charleton (1619–1707),

President of the Royal College of Physicians. In his *Darkness of Atheism* (1652), Charleton argued that just as God had made nature, so could God alter it at will. To prove this divine ability to change the order of nature, he alluded to biblical miracles like the Flood and the eclipse of the sun at Christ's death and held that God could similarly intervene in the future if God so wished. More and more in the course of the seventeenth century, however, the realm of nature was understood to be one of unchangeable, impersonal laws. Thus, another of Boyle's contemporaries, Sir Kenelm Digby (1603–65), found no place for miraculous interventions or other manifestations of particular providence. For him, providence was purely and simply the Creator's original plan, all of whose effects were divinely foreseen. In his critique of Thomas Browne's *Religio Medici,* Digby wrote that "in truth there is no fortuitousness or contingency of things in respect of themselves, but only in respect of us, that are ignorant of their certain and necessary causes."[10] A verbally different but substantially similar position was held by the plant physiologist Nehemiah Grew (1641–1712), who was quite willing to speak of miracles but who reduced them to the level of material events, "natural effects" that were incorporated into the machinery of the original creation just as were less extraordinary phenomena. He could therefore write that "as the asserting of miracles does not derogate from the wisdom of the creation nor the majesty of the Creator, so neither does the intervening of natural causes overthrow miracles."[11]

Most of the virtuosi did not go this far. They generally agreed with Charleton that God could and did still directly intervene in the course of nature, but they insisted more and more frequently that God would do so only on rare and important occasions. This solution to the question of how to reconcile a conception of divine providence with a mechanistic view of nature is evident in the work of the most influential of all the virtuosi, Isaac Newton (1642–1727). His emphasis on "general providence" is clear in the General Scholium that concludes the *Philosophiae Naturalis Principia Mathematica,* where he writes that "this most beautiful system of the sun, planets, and comets could only proceed from the counsel and dominion of an intelligent and powerful Being. . . . This Being governs all things, not as the soul of the world but as Lord over all; and on account of his dominion he is wont to be called *Lord God*."[12] Nevertheless, this dominion as expressed in the original creation required fine tuning from time to time to correct aberrations in the cosmic machine. Although this drew down upon the English scientist the scorn of Gottfried Wilhelm von Leibniz, who insisted in an exchange of letters with Newton's defender Samuel Clarke that necessary interventions of this sort implied a lack of skill in the original work of the Creator, Newton's position that God occasionally intervened in the realm of mechanistic nature was in accord with that of almost all the other virtuosi. In subsequent centuries, there would be many scientists and theologians who concluded that this was an unacceptable compromise solution to what one historian of science has called "the major problem that the scientific theories of the seventeenth century posed for Christian beliefs: the reconciliation of providence and miracles with the mechanistic natural order."[13] There is, however, no doubt but that the virtuosi themselves felt that they had successfully shown how their scientific theories were compatible with their Christian faith in a benevolent, provident God.

Schleiermacher and Barth

During the eighteenth century, such compatibility was not so evident. Thinkers of deistic, pantheistic, or atheistic persuasion offered challenges to traditional Christian theology far more serious than ones it had faced in the immediately preceding period. As John Dillenberger has written, by the middle of the century "the Church was in danger of religious corrosion from within. A new direction was desperately needed."[14] Within the Protestant tradition this direction was first provided by Friedrich Schleiermacher (1768–1834). Of the various issues that led Schleiermacher to explore a new approach to Christian theology, the challenge of modern science was among the most important. The basic ideas of his theology are presented with special clarity in the two open letters he wrote to his friend Friedrich Lücke. In the second of these, Schleiermacher wondered what recent advances in natural science portended for evangelical Christianity. He was unwilling to isolate himself from scientific discoveries, but he then had to ask how long something like the very concept of creation would be able to stand "against the pressure of a worldview formed from scientific inferences that no one can evade."[15] Similarly, he asked how long it would take for the miracles of the New Testament to fall upon the dilemma of either being regarded as part of an entire history that was itself just a fable or else being seen as events analogous to ones that are purely natural.

Schleiermacher's own reformulation of creation and other concepts avoided both a thoroughly supernaturalistic approach, which would assign God to a sphere lying totally outside the scientifically knowable order, and the approach of pantheistic naturalism, by which God's creative work was identified with the causal nexus of nature.[16] Rather, he saw God's causality as different from that found in the natural order but equated with it in extent, the difference arising from the various perspectives or points of view by which humans consider a particular event. He expressed this with all possible clarity in his major work, *The Christian Faith*: "It has always been acknowledged by the strictest dogmaticians that divine preservation, as the absolute dependence of all events and changes on God, and natural causation, as the complete determination of all events by the universal nexus, are one and the same thing *simply from different points of view,* the one being neither separated from the other nor limited by it."[17]

The term "absolute dependence" in the above sentence refers, of course, to that "feeling of absolute dependence" (*das Gefühl der schlechthinnigen Abhängigkeit*) that was for Schleiermacher the characteristic of religion as such, differentiating it from theology (knowledge) on the one hand and morality (action) on the other, though he readily granted that religion had implications for both these other realms. Religious feeling was not something merely subjective but rather, in the words of one scholar, "a revelation of the ultimate ground of reality and consciousness."[18]

This awareness, this consciousness, was for Schleiermacher altogether compatible with a recognition that everything in the natural realm is enclosed within an altogether strict causal nexus of the sort that Leibniz chided Newton for ignoring. The German theologian could thus write that "in each and every situation we ought to be conscious of, and sympathetically experience, absolute dependence on God just as we conceive each and every thing as completely conditioned by the interdependence of nature."[19] Whereas some of his contemporaries said that the advances made by modern science were a threat to religion (and his letter to Friedrich Lücke shows that he himself had sensed this danger), Schleiermacher here claimed just the opposite. Otherwise, "as our knowledge of the world grew perfect, the development of the pious self-consciousness in ordinary life would cease; which is quite contrary to our presupposition that piety is of the essence of human nature."[20] Accordingly, he argued that it would be wrong to conclude that religious feeling awakens when one is confronted by whatever appears incomprehensible in the world around us. If "the great natural phenomena produced by elementary forces" (presumably he meant phenomena like thunderstorms and volcanoes) help awaken that feeling, it is nevertheless not the case that the feeling is weakened or destroyed by attempts to explain such events scientifically. To be sure, it is "an expedient often adopted by human indolence to attribute what is not understood to the supernatural immediately; but this does not at all belong to the tendency to piety."[21] There was, then, in Schleiermacher an ineluctable refusal to attribute to God's direct intervention whatever was not (yet) amenable to scientific understanding, an expedient that in our own day is often referred to as an appeal to "the God of the gaps." As his biographer Martin Redeker writes, for Schleiermacher "the supernaturalistic solution to the dilemma which finds God's omnipotence mainly in the gaps of the natural order or misinterprets his omnipotence as arbitrary intervention in the natural order is impossible."[22]

From the foregoing it is obvious that the miraculous could not have in Schleiermacher's thought even the minimal significance that it had for Robert Boyle and many of his contemporaries. Already in his early work *On Religion* he held that "miracle is simply the religious name for event. Every event, even the most natural and usual, becomes a miracle as soon as the religious view of it can be the dominant. To me all is miracle. In your sense the inexplicable and strange alone is miracle. The more religious you are, the more miracle would you see everywhere."[23] There could, in any case, be no unambiguous manifestation of an "absolutely supernatural" intervention of God in this world, for what is apparently inexplicable today may be able to be explained scientifically tomorrow: "Since our knowledge of created nature is continually growing, we have not the least right to maintain that anything is impossible."[24] On the related topic of the efficacy of prayer, Schleiermacher noted that for many people prayer "seems really to be heard only when because of it an event happens which would not otherwise have happened." Not unexpectedly, he would have nothing to do with such an understanding. Rather, "prayer and its fulfillment or refusal are only part of the original divine plan, and consequently the idea that otherwise something else might have happened is wholly meaningless."[25]

Schleiermacher's approach to issues raised by modern science influenced generations of theologians in the liberal Protestant tradition, who accordingly did not experience the dismay that more traditional Christians felt when confronted with Darwin's theory of evolution a quarter century after Schleiermacher's death. The latter's legacy was not seriously challenged until early in the twentieth century, when Karl Barth (1886–1968) took a radically different starting point from that of "the feeling of absolute dependence." What initiated the break was not, however, a difference on the conceptual level but rather certain events connected with the First World War. In an autobiographical essay that Barth wrote toward the end of his life, he recounted his dismay at seeing, shortly after the outbreak of the war, that among the ninety-three German intellectuals who had issued a manifesto identifying themselves with the war policy of Kaiser Wilhelm II there were numbered almost all the theologians who had taught him. While

Barth was convinced that Schleiermacher, if still alive, would not have signed, "nevertheless, it was still the case that the entire theology which had unmasked itself in that manifesto . . . was grounded, determined, and influenced decisively by him."[26] Specifically, Barth objected to "the consciously and consistently executed anthropological starting point" of Schleiermacher's thought, which "made the christianly pious person into the criterion and content of his theology."[27] In this theology, according to Barth, "nothing remained of the belief that the Word or statement is as such the bearer, bringer, and proclaimer of truth, that there might be such a thing as the Word of God."[28]

As regards the relationship between theology and science, Barth's approach was accordingly different from that of Schleiermacher and the liberal theologians influenced by him, for the Swiss theologian moved deliberately into "the world of the Bible" and from that standpoint saw no need to deal with questions of natural science. Unlike other twentieth-century theologians such as Wolfhart Pannenberg or Karl Rahner, Barth had little knowledge of the natural sciences and gave no indication that he considered such knowledge to be of much significance for theology. In the preface to the "Doctrine of Creation" in his *Church Dogmatics,* he wrote: "There can be no scientific problems, objections or aids in relation to what Holy Scripture and the Christian Church understand by the divine work of creation."[29] Commenting on this attitude, the Barth scholar Harold Nebelsick, who is generally in accord with the teaching of his mentor, expresses regret that this stance in fact meant that by explaining creation on the basis of an ancient Hebrew "saga," Barth not only was kept from engaging questions about creation that arise in our own day but also was overlooking the fact that the Hebrew story was itself based on what people of that era considered a valid cosmogony. Nebelsick concludes: "The point is, theology and science have been so intermingled from the beginning, and certainly from the beginning of the Hellenistic world, . . . that to ignore the discussion with today's science is simply to discuss theology in terms that are related to the science of the by-gone era."[30] It is certainly not the case that Barth would have had no ready opportunity for such discussion. Although warmly invited to attend the conversations between theologians and physicists that were held periodically in Göttingen between the years 1949 and 1961, he always declined the invitations, apparently because he still thought of the natural sciences as they were in previous centuries. In fact, the understanding of science held by Werner Heisenberg and others who attended the Göttingen conversations was more in accord with Barth's own theological method than he would have thought.[31]

Teilhard and Rahner

A radically different approach to the natural sciences on the part of a Christian thinker was that of Pierre Teilhard de Chardin (1881–1955). Born in the Auvergne, he showed a keen interest in natural history from his earliest years. Having entered the Jesuit Order while still in his teens, his studies in paleontology and geology prepared him for what seemed likely to be a lifelong academic career in Paris, but when some of his avant-garde theological ideas came to the attention of his superiors he was asked to spend some time doing paleontological work at a Jesuit school in northern China. What he first thought would be a short period of "exile" stretched into decades, during which time he not only wrote dozens of papers for scientific journals but also composed philosophical and theological essays that led to further difficulties with religious authorities in France and Rome, until he was finally forbidden, in 1948, to engage in any public theological or philosophical speculation. It was, then, only after the posthumous publication of such works as *The Phenomenon of Man* and *The Divine Milieu* that he came to the widespread attention of non-scientists throughout the world.[32]

In fundamental respects Teilhard's approach to the natural sciences was very different from the approaches of Schleiermacher and Barth. Unlike both of them, Teilhard actually practiced a scientific discipline, and from within his paleontological investigations he claimed that he could discern a direction in the whole movement of evolution on earth. In his terminology, the progression was from the realm of inanimate matter ("the geosphere") to that of living organisms ("the biosphere") and from there to that of human beings with their reflective consciousness and freedom ("the noosphere"). On the basis of this past development over billions of years, he went on to extrapolate something about the future, for there was, he believed, no reason to hold that the current of evolution has reached an end. For reasons that were perhaps based as much on intuition as on experimental evidence, Teilhard was convinced that the human species in particular is converging. Signs of cooperation among peoples and nations in the political, scientific, artistic, and religious arenas led him to posit a movement toward what he called the Omega point, the point at which humanity will ultimately reach its maximum degree of complexity, consciousness, and organic unity.

If Teilhard had confined his reflections simply to this area of what he called "the phenomenology of the cosmic" — trying to understand the world as a whole simply as it presents itself to any insightful observer, regardless of the latter's religious convictions or lack thereof — he would no doubt have elicited a certain amount of interest in intellectual circles but would never have emerged as the widely read and controversial thinker that he did in fact become. He once described himself as being not only "a child of earth" (owing to his scientific studies) but also as "a child of heaven" (owing to his religious upbringing, first under the tutelage of his mother and later as a member of the Society of Jesus). Determined not to erect any barrier between these two facets of his life, he struggled hard to bring his phenomenology of the cosmic into line with his understanding of Christian doctrine, especially as found in those Pauline texts that speak of Christ as the one in whom "all the fullness [of God] was pleased to dwell" (Col. 1:19–20) or as the one whom God "has made the head over all things for the church" (Eph. 1:22). For Teilhard, these and similar passages in the New Testament pointed to the conclusion that the movement toward the Omega point was in fact a movement toward the total Christ. As might have been expected, many readers of his works were strongly attracted to the way in which he allowed his scientific studies to enhance his understanding of God's plan for humankind, while others felt that he had forged unwarranted bonds between two realms that should have remained separate, thereby compromising his work as both a scientist and a religious thinker.[33]

Definitely influenced by Teilhard's work (even though he quoted him infrequently) was his fellow Jesuit Karl Rahner (1904–84), whom many consider the most influential Roman Catholic theologian of the twentieth century. While not a practitioner of the natural sciences as was Teilhard, Rahner nevertheless showed a keen interest in scientific questions from the earliest years of his scholarly career and regularly took part in dialogues between theologians and scientists. One of the volumes of his *Theological Investigations* is devoted exclusively to issues in the field of science and religion, while other volumes in the series contain significant essays on such topics.[34] Unlike Barth, Rahner clearly felt called upon to address specific issues raised for Christian faith by modern science. He did so, however, precisely as a theologian — and one whose understanding of God was strongly influenced by what some patristic, medieval, and modern theologians had written about the incomprehensibility of God. Rahner (perhaps influenced by Hegel) often emphasized that our very awareness of ourselves as finite is possible only against the background (or horizon) of what is infinite and unbounded. In an essay from the late 1960s, for example, he wrote: "The moment we become aware of ourselves precisely *as* the limited being which in so many and such radical ways we are, we have already overstepped these boundaries. . . . We have experienced ourselves as beings which constantly reach out beyond themselves toward that which cannot be comprehended or circumscribed, . . . that which is sheer mystery."[35] This last term, "mystery" (or "Absolute Mystery"), was one of Rahner's favored expressions for God, more and more frequently used by him as he grew older. He knew that the best theologians in the history of the Church — like Gregory of Nyssa in the patristic era or Thomas Aquinas in medieval times — were well aware of God's ultimate incomprehensibility, but he also pointed out that this truth had been too little *lived* in earlier centuries. The reason for this lack, he felt, was largely due to the pre-Copernican world view, according to which the universe "was so unassuming and easily surveyed that practically in every direction its limit was quickly reached; it was imaginatively constructed with its spatial and temporal dimensions in such a way that for concrete experience God became almost something like a part of the world, . . . [which] offered in its events, almost at every moment, happenings in which God seemed to be palpably at work."[36] Nowadays, on the contrary, our awareness of living in a cosmos of strictly unimaginable dimensions, in which our very galaxy, itself immense, is but one of billions, can readily lead to a feeling of vertigo, of being "lost" in a seemingly godless expanse. In fact, however, this new situation is a gain, for the cosmos has thereby become "more theological" in the sense of pointing more inexorably than ever before to the immensity of the Creator and our infinite qualitative difference from God as God's creatures. For this reason, said Rahner, "the academic of today has the duty, which is at once pain and grace, of accepting this realization, of not suppressing it in a hasty and cheap apologetic for an anthropomorphic 'belief in God'. . . . We cannot discover God ruling in this world of ours quite so naively as was done in former times. We cannot do this, not because God is dead, but because God is greater, more nameless, more in the background, more incomprehensible."[37]

Of the specific issues that Rahner addressed in his writings on science and religion, one in particular should be mentioned here since it relates to what we have seen in earlier writers like Boyle, Newton, and Schleiermacher. This is the matter of how to conceive of God's action in a world whose events can appear to be part of a strict causal nexus. Should we speak of "special interventions of God" that seem to interrupt this nexus? Should we take advantage of what, since the advent of quantum mechanics, seems to be an "opening" for divine activity at the sub-atomic level, where there is apparently no deterministic nexus anyway? Rahner addressed this sort of issue in his last major work, *Foundations of Chris-*

tian Faith, in the context of the working of divine grace on the human person. If someone, for example, is inspired by "a good idea," there is, on the one hand, the possibility and even the obligation of tracing it back to associations with other ideas, to one's physiological or psychological constitution, and so forth, in such a way that the "good idea" can appear to be utterly determined by past events in the natural order (a position held without further ado by strict determinists like Sigmund Freud). From this perspective, there would seem to be no possibility of being freely open to respond to God's inspiring one to act in a certain way. This viewpoint, limited to what Rahner would term the "categorial" realm of space and time, is not, however, the only one possible. The recipient of the "good idea" could also experience himself or herself as a "transcendental" subject oriented ultimately toward God as the incomprehensible mystery enveloping all of creation, and from this perspective one could apprehend the good idea as having positive, God-inspired significance within the unfolding of one's entire life. To the possible objection that from this perspective *anything* could be viewed as a special intervention by God, Rahner simply asks, "Why, then, may this not be the case?"[38] Rahner's position about the pivotal significance of perspective was thus similar to that of Schleiermacher, however much the two theologians would have disagreed on other points.

Looking Back and Ahead

This overview of some central figures and issues in science and religion since the seventeenth century helps make it clear that when contemporary thinkers like Michael Behe and John Haught debate the issue of design they are part of a discussion that has been going on for a long time. Four hundred years ago, scientists like Kepler, Boyle, and Newton were far readier than many today to affirm that the order they found in the world around them gave evidence of a designing, creating God, but even in their time there was considerable disagreement about whether or not God ever did (or still does) intervene in special ways that could be deemed miraculous. We have seen that Boyle and Newton answered this question affirmatively, though with the qualification that such acts were infrequent (and rarer now than in the time of the early church), while Digby, Grew, and Schleiermacher denied this kind of special intervention (though the latter two of them redefined "the miraculous" in ways that permitted the continued use of the term). There was also the question of whether it is desirable for a theologian to be familiar with the findings made and questions posed by natural science. Whereas Barth felt little or no need for this kind of expertise, Teilhard and Rahner deemed it to be a central part of their calling to deal theologically with issues raised in the scientific realm. Teilhard likewise gave strong affirmation to the possibility of discerning an overall direction in the evolutionary story of the universe (and of our planet in particular). As we shall see later in this book, a number of thinkers today agree with the notion of "direction" but have serious disagreements among themselves as to whether "direction" permits one to speak of "design" as well. In general, this kind of debate arises against the background of what it means even to speak of God's action in the world, an issue that will be especially prominent in the chapters dealing with the origin of the universe, evolution, and eschatology. To the first of these topics I now turn.

2

Cosmology and
the Doctrine of Creation

HISTORIANS OF SCIENCE are generally agreed that Albert Einstein was the greatest theoretical physicist of the twentieth century, but what was arguably the most momentous scientific discovery of the century was one that Einstein himself initially would not accept — the expansion of the universe. Contrary to the almost universal opinion of scientists at the time, in the 1920s the Russian astronomer Aleksandr Friedmann and the Belgian mathematician Georges Lemaître, working independently of each other, had reasoned on theoretical grounds that the universe was not static but expanding. Carefully documented experimental evidence for this surmise came toward the end of that decade with the findings of the American astronomers Edwin Hubble and Milton Humason at the Mount Wilson Observatory in California. Already in the mid-1920s and on the basis of meticulous examination of photographic studies of the night sky, Hubble had determined that many of the nebulae ("clouds") detectable in the night sky were not within the Milky Way (which was at that time believed to be the whole of the universe) but were galaxies in their own right. Hubble and Humason further detected that the light emitted from these galaxies was shifted toward the red end of the spectrum. The most widely accepted interpretation of this red shift ascribes it to the Doppler Effect, meaning that the longer wave lengths associated with that end of the spectrum are due to the receding of the galaxies from one another as well as from observers on earth. For this reason, a large majority of contemporary astronomers have concluded that at some point in the very distant past (perhaps fifteen billion years

29

ago) the present universe took its origin from what is known as a singularity, a point sometimes described as being of "infinite density and zero volume." Some theologians and religious thinkers have taken this event (commonly called "the big bang") to be the moment of creation referred to at the beginning of the Book of Genesis and elsewhere in the Bible.

One of the best-known assertions of this connection between modern cosmology and religious doctrine was made by Pope Pius XII in an address to the Pontifical Academy of Sciences on 22 November 1951. After stating his wish to give his hearers a summary of "the priceless services rendered by modern science to the demonstration of the existence of God,"[1] the pope went on to give brief descriptions of various scientific discoveries, including those of Hubble. While admitting that such discoveries did not provide absolute proof of creation in time, he came very close to such a conclusion by claiming that

> with that concreteness which is characteristic of physical proofs, it [modern science] has confirmed the contingency of the universe and also the well-founded deduction as to the epoch when the cosmos came forth from the hands of the Creator.
>
> Hence, creation took place in time. Therefore, there is a Creator. Therefore, God exists! Although it is neither explicit nor complete, this is the reply we were awaiting from science, and which the present human generation is awaiting from it.[2]

Even at the time, some (including Lemaître, himself a Catholic priest) felt that the pope's conclusion was unwarranted, and it is noteworthy that Pope John Paul II, some thirty years later, was much more cautious in referring to the same scientific findings. In an address to the Pontifical Academy of Sciences on 3 October 1981, he said:

> Any scientific hypothesis on the origin of the world, such as the hypothesis of a primitive atom from which derived the whole of the physical universe, leaves open the problem

concerning the universe's beginning. Science cannot of itself solve this question. There is needed that human knowledge that rises above physics and astrophysics and which is called metaphysics; there is needed above all the knowledge that comes from God's revelation.[3]

Still others have not merely avoided Pius XII's assertion of a close connection between contemporary cosmogony and a doctrine of divine creation but have even claimed that if the universe took its origin from a singularity, then this is incompatible with the existence of God. The atheistic philosopher Quentin Smith builds on Stephen Hawking's assertion that any emissions from such a singularity would be completely unpredictable, since the classical concepts of space and time break down at that point. We should then, argues Smith, "expect a totally chaotic outpouring from it,"[4] and this he finds altogether incompatible with belief in a provident God.

It is obvious, then, that modern cosmology has given rise to reflections on religious issues but that these reflections have shown the greatest diversity. The rest of this chapter will first consider in further detail some contemporary theories about the origin of the universe and will then move on to a consideration of what, if anything, these theories have to say about the existence of a Creator.

Current Theories about the Origin of the Universe

As noted above, the most commonly accepted cosmological theory today holds that our universe took its origin in a singularity some fifteen billion years ago. One of the main reasons offered in support of this theory is that the red shift detected in the light spectra of distant galaxies indicates that they are now generally moving away from one another (apart from some local areas where the force of gravity draws several galaxies together in massive collisions). A second argument is based on the work of Robert Wilson and Arno Penzias in the mid-1960s. For some time previously it had been predicted that if the universe were rapidly expanding from an initial singularity, some evidence of that massive event should still be detectable. Working on a different project at the Bell Laboratories in New Jersey, the two physicists discovered a faint microwave radiation coming from all directions in the universe and having a temperature of about 2.7°K, a figure consistent with the predicted value. This was widely understood by scientists to give very strong confirmation to the theory. Further support for it is based on the existence of certain elements in the universe (these being determined by the examination of light spectra), for the observed abundance of hydrogen, helium, deuterium, and lithium and their relative proportions are in accord with what the theory predicts.

One problem that the theory faced for some decades was the difficulty of explaining how galaxies could have formed if the expansion was precisely uniform and homogeneous, as seemed to be indicated by the uniform temperature of the background radiation. This difficulty was overcome by the more exact measurements of the Cosmic Background Explorer satellite (COBE) in the early 1990s, for it detected minute differences in the background temperature that seemed significant enough to account for the relative "lumpiness" of the early universe and the eventual formation of galaxies.

These are the major arguments in support of the theory of the big bang. By correlating the findings of astronomers and astrophysicists working on the scale of the very large and those of particle physicists dealing with the very small, cosmologists have tried to determine something of the history of the expansion after the big bang. The details of this theory have been discussed at length in books and articles written for specialists as well as ones intended for a more general audience.[5] For our present purposes it is not necessary to go into great detail, but a brief summary of these cosmologists' ideas would be in order. They speculate that within unimaginably small fractions of a second after the expansion the four basic forces of nature (gravitation, the strong and weak nuclear forces, and the electromagnetic force) began to separate from their primal unity. Immediately thereafter were formed subatomic particles, later came atoms and molecules, and after about one billion years stars and galaxies appeared. After another nine billion years planets emerged in some star systems, including our own solar system, and several billion years after that came the first appearance of life on our planet, with organisms composed of elements that had originally been formed in the depths of stars and then propelled into space in supernovae explosions.

If "explosion" is the correct term in the case of supernovae, it is, on the other hand, misleading when speaking about the rapid expansion from the initial singularity. Despite the universal and somewhat regrettable terminology of "the big bang," the expansion should not be thought of as the explosive bursting forth of primordial matter into an enveloping space; rather, scientists understand the big bang to have involved the expansion of space itself. The nature of the initial singularity is itself prone to various kinds of misunderstanding. At that point the four basic physical forces had not yet separated out from one another, meaning that the known laws of physics were not applicable. Although one may get the impression from popular texts that scientists feel able to speculate just how the universe evolved from the singularity itself, this is not actually the case. Even the most tentative speculations reach back only to the so-called Planck time of 10^{-43} second, the time at which the gravitational force is thought to have separated. Anything that happened before then exceeds the limits of the theory. Accordingly the astronomer William Stoeger cautions that the initial singularity "is not an origin or a beginning in an absolute sense — but only within the context of the model — and any possible state prior to the singularity is inaccessible to us. Long before reaching it, in fact, we gradually lose our ability to make observations or perform experiments which directly test these extreme epochs."[6] For this reason, it seems preferable to refer to the singularity not as an "event" within our four-dimensional space-time continuum but rather as a boundary or edge of this continuum, "an epistemological boundary to the domain where the Big Bang theory can be trusted."[7]

Despite this limit, most scientists are confident that information gleaned from elementary particle theory and from quantum theory in general allows them to know a great deal about conditions in the very early universe. As they conducted this kind of research in the last half of the twentieth century, some unexpected results emerged from their work, for in study after study it seemed that if conditions had been even slightly different from what they were, then our life-bearing universe would not have evolved. Of the many factors that are regularly discussed in this connection, one of the more striking concerns the balance between the force of expansion emanating from the big bang and driving matter apart and the force of gravity drawing matter together. At the above-mentioned Planck time, it is commonly reckoned that these two forces were so closely balanced that they differed from each other by only one part in 10^{60}. The physicist-theologian John Polkinghorne has tried to emphasize the enormity of that figure by noting that if one took a target an inch wide and placed it on the other side of the observable universe and then took aim and hit the target, one would have attained an accuracy of one in 10^{60}.[8] If the force of expansion had dominated by just a bit more than this, it is calculated that matter would have expanded too rapidly for stars and galaxies to form, whereas if the force of contraction had been just slightly stronger, then the universe would have collapsed back in on itself before matter could have coalesced in any interesting way. Commenting on this and a number of similar figures, Ernan McMullin concludes: "To get a life-bearing universe requires one to set very precise constraints on its initial state; to use a metaphor that has since become famous, it has to be 'fine-tuned.' "[9] Not surprisingly, a number of thinkers — scientists as well as philosophers and theologians — feel that this apparent fine tuning points to a divine Fine Tuner. Since the eventual appearance of our species seems in some sense to have been planned, the entire set of these apparently fine-tuned constraints is commonly called the anthropic principle, though some commentators caution that they are referring only to the likelihood that intelligence in *some* form would eventually appear in the universe, not necessarily in the form characteristic of *Homo sapiens*. However, as we shall see later in this chapter, other thinkers find no theistic implications at all in these data.

A number of those scientists who find no theological import in the anthropic principle are likewise unconvinced by the big bang theory itself. Foremost among them was Fred Hoyle, the British scientist who coined the term "big bang" by speaking derisively of it in a radio talk on the BBC in 1950. The term stuck, despite a sense on the part of some that it is not very satisfactory. Indeed, when *Sky and Telescope* magazine sponsored a contest in 1993 to come up with a better name, none of the more than 13,000 entries was judged better! Hoyle's alternative theory was that of a steady-state universe, no doubt advocated by him not simply on scientific grounds but also because he sensed that the big bang theory implied a Creator, an implication unacceptable to someone who had once written that "religion is but a desperate attempt to find an escape from the truly dreadful situation in which we find ourselves."[10]

More ambiguous on the question of an initial singularity is the well-known Cambridge physicist Stephen Hawking, who certainly does not hold Hoyle's theory of a steady state universe but who has nevertheless moved away from the notion that big bang cosmology requires an absolute beginning in time. Hawking's thought is still developing, but at least at the time he published his best-selling book *A Brief History of Time* he argued that there is no boundary condition for either space or time but only a curved spacetime that does not take us back to a point of absolute zero before which there was no time. In his oft-quoted words, the universe would then "be completely self-contained and not affected by anything outside itself. It would neither be created or destroyed. It would just BE."[11]

Other cosmologists, likewise objecting to the notion that the universe had an absolute beginning in time, have suggested that the big bang at the origin of our present universe is only one of countless expansions that have been going on in an oscillating universe that expands and contracts endlessly, while still others

surmise that there may be numerous universes existing simultaneously, with ours just happening to be one in which conditions
allowed for the development of life and consciousness.[12]

Those who advocate the "classical" big bang theory find serious problems with all of these competing theories. Actually few
scientists still accept the steady state theory, not least because
it (at least in Hoyle's formulation) would require the continual
creation of hydrogen atoms and there has been absolutely no experimental confirmation of such an occurrence. Hawking's attempt
to rid spacetime of its initial singularity requires his introduction
of "imaginary time," correlative to the notion of imaginary numbers in mathematics. Hawking writes, for example: "In imaginary
time, there are no singularities or boundaries. So maybe what we
call imaginary time is really more basic, and what we call real
is just an idea that we invent to help us describe what we think
the universe is like."[13] Hawking is unquestionably a genius in the
field of mathematical physics, but this expertise does not automat-
ically make him a convincing metaphysician. One may well find
his ideas about imaginary time intriguing, but it seems doubtful
that they will find wide acceptance. So, too, as regards the theories
about multiple universes, whether consecutive (as in the oscillating
model) or simultaneous (according to which ours might be but one
of many currently existing). On the one hand, these possibilities
could never be absolutely disproved, but on the other hand there
seems to be no way ever to confirm their existence. While it would
certainly be unwise for theologians and other religious thinkers to
bind themselves too closely to the big bang theory, since no one has
any way of knowing how this theory might evolve or be replaced in
decades or centuries to come, it is certainly the one that has gained
broadest acceptance among cosmologists today. If theology is to be
true to the interdisciplinary character that has always marked it at
its best, then it is incumbent on at least some theologians to reflect
seriously on what this particular cosmological theory holds. In the
words of Arthur Peacocke, who is both a respected biochemist and
a widely read Anglican theologian, "any affirmation about God's
relation to the world of creation, if it is not to become vacuous and

sterile, must be about the relation of God to, [and] the creation by God of, the world which the natural sciences describe. It seems to me that this is not a situation where Christian, or indeed any, theology has a choice."[14] Likewise, William Stoeger has written that "it is important for the theologian to take into consideration what cosmology, and science in general, reveals to us of the universe and our place in it.... Certainly, at least in some way, such a perspective and such understanding enriches theological reflection and provides *some* of the detailed experiential points of reference from which we consider who God is, and who He is not, and who we are in relation to Him, to one another, and to our world."[15] It is in the spirit of Peacocke's and Stoeger's words that the theological reflections in the remaining part of this chapter have been composed.

The Doctrine of Creation in Scripture and in the Patristic and Medieval Eras

The roots of the Christian doctrine of creation lie in many parts of the Hebrew Bible, including hymnic passages like Psalm 104 with its praise of God who "spread out the heavens like a tent-cloth" and "fixed the earth upon its foundation, not to be moved forever" (Ps. 104:2, 5) and God's powerful and lengthy questioning Job out of the storm: "Where were you when I founded the earth?...Have you fitted a curb to the Pleiades or loosened the bonds of Orion?...Do you give the horse his strength and endow his neck with splendor? Do you make the steed to quiver, while his thunderous snorting spreads terror?" (Job 38:4, 31; 39:19–20). These, and similar passages in some of the prophetic books, provide rich imagery for the doctrine of creation, including that ongoing divine preservation of the world known technically as *creatio continua*.

There is, however, no doubt but that the most widely discussed biblical text about creation is the opening of the Book of Genesis. Its first verse has frequently been translated into English as "In the beginning God created heaven or earth" (or some slight variation of these words), reflecting the Greek Septuagint's *En archē epoiēsen ho theos ton ouranon kai tēn gēn* and the Latin Vulgate's *In principio creavit Deus caelum et terram.* Recent scriptural scholarship, however, has argued that the opening words in the Hebrew text cannot syntactically be so translated. Thus Richard Clifford and Roland Murphy, noting parallels with other biblical and Near Eastern cosmogonies, translate instead: "When God began to create heaven and earth — the earth being formless and void, with darkness over the surface of the deep, and a wind of God sweeping over the waters — then God said, 'Let there be light,' and there was light."[16] Similarly, E. A. Speiser renders the passage as follows: "When God set about to create heaven and earth — the world being then a formless waste, with darkness over the seas and only an awesome wind sweeping over the water — God said, 'Let there be light.' And there was light."[17] The difference between these and the more traditional rendering may appear to be slight, but the newer translations do render less certain the longstanding conviction that the opening verses of the Bible clearly taught a temporal beginning of the universe. One could possibly interpret these verses as implying an already existing earth — formless, void, and dark — with the creative action being that of introducing light, order, and eventually living beings into a scene of primal chaos.

A further point regularly noted by modern commentators is that the Hebrew verb *bara'*, translated above as "create," is regularly used in the Bible only when God is the subject, whereas the verb *'asah* ("make") is used with either God or human beings as subject. "Making" is thus analogous to human "manufacture," by which an object is fashioned so as to receive its particular character, whereas "creating" is not comparable to what humans can do.[18] God alone could "create" heaven and earth, whatever this activity might mean more exactly.

In fact, it did not take long within the Christian era for speculation to begin about the precise meaning of "create," for early Christian writers had to combat Gnostic dualism on the one hand and pantheism on the other. Both heresies had at least one point in common: that matter was in some sense eternal. For the dual-

ists, reality was made up of two very different kinds of elements —
formal principles that gave shape to things, and material elements
that received the shaping — and both had existed from all eternity. Almost from the beginning, Christian writers opposed an
understanding of reality in which matter, as over against a form-
giving God, was equally fundamental and primary, for this was
judged to derogate from the divine sovereignty. Thus Tatian, a
second-century apologist of Syrian origin, taught that matter was
generated directly by God, for if ungenerated it would be a second
principle, in some respects equal to God.[19] In the same century,
Theophilus of Antioch argued explicitly against the eternity of the
world. After commending Plato and his followers for acknowledging that God is unbegotten, he went on to criticize them for
holding that matter is also uncreated and therefore coeval with
God: "If God is uncreated and matter is uncreated, then, according to the Platonists, God is no longer the Creator of all things."
Moreover, "what great thing would it be if God made the world
out of existing matter? Even a human artist, when he obtains material from someone, makes of it whatever he pleases. But the power
of God is made evident in this, that He makes out of what does
not exist whatever He pleases, and the giving of life and movement
belongs to none other, but to God alone."[20] Irenaeus of Lyons,
the most important Christian theologian of the second century,
made the same point when he wrote: "Humans, indeed, are not
able to make something from nothing, but only from existing material. God, however, is greater than humans first of all in this:
that when nothing existed beforehand, He called into existence
the very material for His creation."[21] Such texts, and similar ones
from Tertullian, contributed significantly to the Christian doctrine
of creation out of nothing, *creatio ex nihilo*. Augustine of Hippo,
the greatest theologian in the Western church during the patristic
era, pondered the question of creation at still greater length than
any of the theologians just mentioned. His reflections on creation
and time in book eleven of his *Confessions* are still regularly cited
by philosophers, above all his insight that it is pointless to ask what
God was doing before he made heaven and earth, since time itself

was created at that point: "It is therefore true to say that when you had not made anything, there was no time, because time itself was of your making. And no time is co-eternal with you, because you never change; whereas, if time never changed, it would not be time."[22]

In those early Christian centuries, then, any teaching about the eternity of matter was roundly condemned. In the Middle Ages, it was even thought by some theologians, such as Bonaventure, that one could prove philosophically that the world had a beginning in time. His still more influential contemporary, Thomas Aquinas, disagreed, and Thomas's position is now widely accepted. His basic argument is that the articles of faith cannot be proved demonstratively and that God's creation of the world is clearly such an article — is, in fact, the very first article of the creed: "I believe in one God, the Father almighty, creator of heaven and earth." Therefore the temporal beginning or "newness of the world" (*novitas mundi*) can be known only by revelation. For Thomas such revelation is manifest in the very first words of the Bible, which he quotes from the Vulgate: *In principio creavit Deus caelum et terram.* His answer is accordingly clear and concise: "By faith alone do we hold, and by no demonstration can it be proved, that the world did not always exist."[23]

Some Contemporary Thinkers on the Doctrine of Creation and the Anthropic Principle

In his reply to one of the objections to this position, Thomas notes that even some who (like the Islamic philosopher Avicenna) claim that the world is eternal nevertheless do not reject the word "creation," understanding the term to mean that the world "was not made from something else" (*non est factus de aliquo*).[24] This comment points to a distinction that is regularly found among theologians and philosophers who write about creation in our own day. Although most people probably understand God's creation of the world to imply that the latter had an absolute temporal beginning (sometimes called "historical/empirical origination"), in the most fundamental sense creation means only the dependence of the world upon God ("ontological origination").[25] Emphasizing the latter meaning, Arthur Peacocke writes: "The principal stress in the Judeo-Christian doctrine of creation ... is on the dependence and contingency of all entities, and events, other than God himself: it is about a personal relationship between God and the world and not about the beginning of the Earth, or the whole universe, at a point in time."[26] Keith Ward, Regius Professor of Theology at the University of Oxford, states similarly that "it is irrelevant to a doctrine of creation *ex nihilo* whether the universe began or not; that the universe began was usually accepted because of a particular reading of Genesis 1. The doctrine of creation *ex nihilo* simply maintains that there is nothing other than God from which the universe is made, and that the universe is other than God and wholly dependent upon God for its existence."[27] The distinction drawn by Peacocke and Ward is important for the science-religion dialogue, for it indicates that a theology of creation need not be wedded to a cosmological theory that has the universe beginning in (or with) time. Although it is difficult to see how the existence of an eternal, oscillating universe could ever be scientifically confirmed, even the possibility of its existence would not pose problems for theologians like the two just mentioned.

For other theologians, however, the note of "historical/empirical origination" is far more important, even though they, too, recognize the possibility of distinguishing this from creation in the sense of ontological dependence. Jürgen Moltmann, for example, fears that if the notion of *creatio ex nihilo* were simply reduced to the giving of form to a not-yet-actualized primordial matter, "then the world process must be just as eternal and without any beginning as God himself." This, he alleges, would lead to pantheism, for the world process would then "be one of God's natures. And in this case we have to talk about 'the divinization of the world'. God and nature are fused into a unified world process."[28] Ted Peters is likewise wary of attempts to emphasize creation as ontological dependence at the expense of creation as implying a temporal beginning: "Why are we so quick to give up the idea of an initial origin?...To reduce *creatio ex nihilo* to a vague commitment about the dependence of the world upon God — though accurate — does not help much. It simply moves the matter to a higher level of abstraction. We still need to ask: just what does it mean for the world to owe its existence to God? One sensible answer is this: had God not acted to bring the spacetime world into existence, there would be only nothing."[29] Retaining the emphasis on "an initial origin," he feels, is consonant with discussions already taking place within scientific cosmology and therefore offers theology an opportunity for fruitful dialogue with science.

Such differences between Peacocke and Ward on the one hand and Moltmann and Peters on the other as regards the doctrine of creation are paralleled by disagreements among other thinkers concerning the possible theological significance of the anthropic principle. In discussing this particular issue, unlike discussion of the doctrine of creation itself, there is no need to go back to pre-twentieth century authors, since the measurements that have given rise to the principle are so recent. The extremely fine balance between the forces of expansion and contraction in the universe was mentioned earlier in this chapter as one of the factors that gave rise to this principle. Numerous others have been offered, including the following as a representative sample:

- If the strong nuclear force were just slightly weaker, multi-proton nuclei would not hold together; if slightly stronger, the supply of various life-essential elements heavier than iron would not be in sufficient supply.

- If the electromagnetic coupling constant were slightly smaller, no electrons would be held in orbit about their nuclei; if slightly stronger, an atom could not share an electron orbit with other atoms. Either way, there would be no molecules and hence no life.

- If the entropy level for the universe were slightly larger, no galaxies would form; if slightly smaller, the galactic systems that formed would effectively trap radiation and prevent any fragmentation of the systems into stars. In either case, life would not be able to arise.[30]

These and similar data have led a number of scientists to find positive theological implications in the anthropic principle. Thus, the American astronomer George Greenstein surmises: "As we survey all the evidence, the thought insistently arises that some supernatural agency — or, rather, Agency — must be involved. . . . Was it God who stepped in and so providentially crafted the cosmos for our benefit?"[31] The mathematical physicist Paul Davies is more nuanced in his reflections but, like Greenstein, he finds pointers toward a Deity in the kinds of facts listed above. He rejects the notion of a God who "selected a design that would achieve an especially desirable end result [such as the evolution of intelligent life] and then set about creating the real thing." Davies does, however, think that "a more subtle notion" of design is in accord with the scientific data. He suggests that "a universe which behaves as if directed towards a goal need not require a Deity who manipulates the specific 'play' of this particular cosmic game. But it is suggestive of a Deity who has selected from the infinite variety of possible rules of the game (i.e., laws) a particular set which facilitates, and possibly even maximizes in some sense, the propensity for the game to develop rich and interesting behavior."[32] Ernan McMullin similarly notes that "the most obvious way to convert the anthropic principle into a properly explanatory (but no longer strictly 'scientific') one is to suppose that the 'fine-tuning' is the work of a Creator who in some sense 'intends' life to develop in the way it did."[33]

Other scholars, however, find no theological implications whatever in the anthropic principle. Representative of this position is the British philosopher Nicholas Bostrum, who argues that the anthropic principle "holds out the prospect of an alternative explanation of why the universe appears to be 'fine-tuned' for life, an explanation that does not invoke a Designer. Rather, the idea is that . . . our universe is but one in a vast ensemble of universes.

If these universes have randomly different values of their fundamental physical constants and other parameters, then just by chance a few of them will be life-permitting."[34] One such universe, of course, would be ours. Other thinkers who are professedly religious are nevertheless suspicious about attempts to use the anthropic principle for theological purposes, primarily because it is impossible to say that there will never be natural, scientific explanations for what currently appear to be remarkable coincidences. Ian Barbour, one of the earliest proponents of the dialogue between science and religion, warns that "perhaps there is a more fundamental theory that will show that the constants can only have the values that they have. In the history of science there have been many apparent coincidences . . . which later received theoretical explanation."[35] Likewise, William Stoeger cautions that many scientists believe that a question such as that of why the fundamental physical constants possess the values they have will eventually prove to be answerable within the fields of physics and cosmology.[36] If this turns out to be the case, then seeing these apparently "fine-tuned" constants as pointing toward a divine Designer would have to be judged as only one more instance of appealing to a "God-of-the-gaps," that is, concluding to divine intervention when no natural explanation lies ready to hand.

Concluding Reflections on These Issues

The foregoing section of this chapter has revealed that there are major disagreements among contemporary thinkers concerning several major theological issues raised by modern cosmology: Does the big bang theory imply the existence of a creator God, and does the apparent fine tuning of the universe from its earliest period point to divine design? How might such questions best be resolved?

To begin, it is important to note that the very methodology of science that has allowed it to make such progress since the seventeenth century has inherent limitations. Science as such deals with empirically verifiable data. The Polish bishop Joseph M. Zycinski, who is also a trained philosopher of science, notes that "the methodological principles of modern physics imply that any physical state S_n should be explained by reference to an earlier state S_{n-1}. For methodological reasons, the scientific series of explanations in the past of the universe should be continued ad infinitum unless one proves that the moment t_0 must be introduced into cosmic history as an 'absolute zero,' much as the absolute zero of temperature must be accepted in Kelvin's scale."[37] But we have already seen that there can apparently be no absolute proof that a singularity at the beginning of our universe corresponds to an absolute beginning of time, since the theory of an oscillating universe, even if itself undemonstrable, remains tenable. For this reason, J. Wentzel van Huyssteen, Professor of Theology and Science at Princeton Theological Seminary, writes that "the why of it all, the ultimate explanation of existence, turns out to be unanswerable in terms of scientific methodology."[38] Similarly, Ted Peters observes: "The scientific method cannot deny the relevance of the Beyond; but it cannot affirm it either.... The Beyond lies outside the perimeter of scientific knowing, and always will."[39]

Peters' comment in particular, with its reference to "the Beyond," correctly implies that the notion of creation is a properly religious one. It is understandable that persons who are already imbued with a religious perspective on the world, such as Pope Pius XII as quoted earlier in this chapter, would readily interpret big bang cosmology in theistic terms, but the way in which he did so will almost inevitably not be convincing to those who do not share that basic perspective. Even in the extremely unlikely case that it could somehow be shown conclusively that our universe originated in "a singular event" that was not preceded by a "big crunch" and that ours is the only universe that is or ever was, this would still not allow cosmology *as such* to demonstrate the existence of a Creator. A non-theistic scientist or philosopher could still say, in the words of the atheist Quentin Smith, that this world "exists nonnecessarily, improbably, and causelessly. It exists *for absolutely no reason at all*. It is *inexplicably* and *stunningly actual*.... The impact of this captivated realization upon me is overwhelming. I am completely stunned."[40]

For this reason, one would surely have to agree with Pope John Paul II who, as we have seen, stipulated that science itself cannot solve the question of the universe's beginning: "There is needed that human knowledge that rises above physics and astrophysics and which is called metaphysics." Among other things, this should caution a theistic philosopher or theologian from relying very closely on particular cosmological theories when pondering the question of creation. The best starting point will not be the big bang theory or the seemingly remarkable data associated with the anthropic principle, but rather the very fact that the universe exists. Joseph Zycinski recalls that in a 1992 interview Stephen Hawking pointed out that even his physical description of a no-boundary universe does not explain why the universe exists at any particular moment of cosmic time. Zycinski comments: "In this profound remark we can find an echo of Leibniz's question, Why is there anything rather than nothing?"[41]

To be sure, one could still say in reply to the Leibnizian question that the existence of the universe is simply a matter of random chance, something inexplicable, causeless, and ultimately pointless. We have seen Quentin Smith holding this position. In another of his works, and in a similar vein, Smith writes: "I find it quite easy to conceive of the universe beginning to exist without a cause.... I find this uncaused beginning astonishing, amazing, 'mind-boggling', and utterly awesome, but that is different from saying I cannot conceive it to be the case."[42] For many, however, including myself, it is philosophically far more adequate to argue that the universe is not causeless. William Lane Craig's critique of Smith's claim is trenchant:

On the theistic view, the potentiality of the universe's existence lay in the power of God to create it. On the atheistic interpretation, on the other hand, there did not even exist any potentiality for the existence of the universe. But then it seems inconceivable that the universe should come to be actual if there did not exist any potentiality for its existence. It seems to me therefore that a little reflection discloses that our mental picture of the universe arising uncaused out of absolutely nothing is just that: pure imagination. Philosophical reflection reveals it to be inconceivable.[43]

To say that the universe is not causeless but that it finds its ultimate source in God is to make a claim for which ineluctable proof cannot be given (otherwise there would be no counter-positions such as that held by Quentin Smith), but it is nevertheless a claim that is reasonable, coherent, and able to be understood as what Keith Ward has called "the completion of that search for intelligibility which characterizes the scientific enterprise."[44] It must be emphasized, however, that a genuinely theological doctrine of creation says something different from and much more comprehensive than what could be deduced from any cosmological theory. The Polish philosopher Michael Heller rightly notes that an historical analysis of the development of this doctrine "shows persuasively that the theological idea of creation is immensely richer than anything physics or cosmology is able to say."[45] It holds not only that every moment of time (and not just some first moment) comes from God's creative power, but also that everything that exists is properly to be viewed within the context of a divine love that brought it into being and maintains it so. This means, as George Ellis points out, that the proper context for reflecting on the "Why?" of creation is not simply that of physics and chemistry but that of "the full nature of our existence, with our fears and hopes, love and caring, value judgments, ethical choices and moral responsibility, whose reality I take to be at least as indubitable as any other area of experience."[46] It is not merely pious sentimentality but respect for the full expanse of human experience to consider creation from this broader perspective, which means taking into account what poets, mystics, and religiously sensitive persons have had to say. Among these would surely be numbered Pierre Teilhard de Chardin, who in the very midst of his paleontological explorations would regularly reflect on the earth and the surrounding universe as God's creation, as when he wrote:

> In the beginning was *Power,* intelligent, loving, energizing. In the beginning was the *Word,* supremely capable of mastering and moulding whatever might come into being in the world of matter. In the beginning there were not coldness and darkness: there was the *Fire.* This is the truth.
>
> So, far from light emerging gradually out of the womb of our darkness, it is the Light existing before all else was made which, patiently, surely, eliminates our darkness. . . . You, my God, are the inmost depths, the stability of that eternal *milieu,* without duration or space, in which our cosmos emerges gradually into being and grows gradually to its final completeness, as it loses those boundaries which to our eyes seem so immense.[47]

The sacramental view of the world evident in those lines from Teilhard are reflected as well in the poetry of someone like Gerard Manly Hopkins, one of whose best-known poems, "God's Grandeur," begins with the lines:

> The world is charged with the grandeur of God.
> It will flame out, like shining from shook foil;
> It gathers to a greatness, like the ooze of oil
> Crushed. Why do men then now not reck his rod?

It is not at all fanciful to suggest that we, living well more than a century after Hopkins's death and far more conversant than he could have been about the immensity of the universe and the complexities of its structure, are in a much more privileged position to sense something of that "grandeur of God" of which he wrote. William Stoeger notes that "material reality is on every level more vast, more intricate in its structure and development, more amazing in its evolution, in its variety flowing from fundamental levels of unity, and in its balance of functions, than we could have imagined without the contributions of the sciences."[48] To have learned this from contemporary cosmology is more conducive to a full appreciation of the doctrine of creation than any particular cosmological theory could be.

3

Evolution and the
Doctrine of Divine Providence

A T THE CONCLUSION of the previous chapter, the priest-astronomer William Stoeger was quoted as referring to the "amazing" character of the evolution of material reality. For religious believers, that adjective has not always been the first to come to mind. "Challenging," "troubling," even "atheistic" are other terms that have been used to describe the theory as proposed by Charles Darwin in *On the Origin of Species by Means of Natural Selection,* first published in 1859. The challenge it presented was not primarily the claim that the human race descended from earlier species (a claim only implicit in *The Origin of Species* and then developed by Darwin in his later book *The Descent of Man* [1871]) but rather the implication that the entire process of evolution was so driven by chance as to be incompatible with belief in a providential God. There was, in other words, a clash of worldviews. From the time of Isaac Newton up to that of Darwin, it had been assumed that mechanical views of a Newtonian type could indeed prevail within the natural sciences of physics, chemistry, astronomy, geology, and the like, but that these were not applicable in the fields of biology, psychology, sociology, and other studies of human behavior. In biology, for example, it was commonly held that divine providence was clearly in control. Eleven years before the publication of *The Origin of Species,* the British anatomist Richard Owen wrote that "the Divine mind which planned the Archetype also foreknew all its modifications. The archetypal idea was manifested ... upon this planet long prior to the existence of those animal species that actually exemplify it."[1] Such a claim, reflecting the compromise between naturalistic and theistic viewpoints that had held since the time of Newton, was jeopardized or even shattered by Darwin's placing biology, too, within "a world of impersonal and purposeless laws."[2]

This certainly does not mean that everyone who understood Darwin's argument concluded that it could not be reconciled with traditional Christian belief in a providential God. Darwin himself ended *The Origin of Species* with the following sentence: "There is grandeur in this view of life; with its several powers having been originally breathed by the Creator into a few forms or into one; and that, whilst this planet has gone cycling on according to the fixed law of gravity, from so simple a beginning endless forms most wonderful and most beautiful have been, and are being evolved." Only later, and largely because of his revulsion over the doctrine of eternal damnation and his personal devastation at the death of his eldest daughter Annie, did Darwin abandon Christianity and adopt the stance of agnosticism.[3]

One early proponent of what is now usually called "theistic evolution" was Frederick Temple, a future archbishop of Canterbury. A year after the publication of Darwin's book, Temple preached the official sermon at the Oxford meeting of the British Association. He argued that God's work was to be discerned within the laws of nature and, according to one observer, he espoused Darwin's ideas fully.[4] Others, however, disagreed, one of the most thorough critiques of Darwinian theory coming from the Princeton theologian Charles Hodge in his book *What Is Darwinism?* (1874). Hodge did not dismiss the theory out of hand, for he admitted that one could, in principle, argue that God directed the development of new species. In fact, however, he said that the theory as presented by Darwin was *effectively* atheistic, since the process of natural selection working on random variations left no evident role for a providential God. Agnostic or atheistic scientists and philosophers both then and now agreed on this point. In the mid-twentieth century, the biologist George Gaylord Simpson stated bluntly that "Darwin destroyed the last stronghold of the supernatural, the providential and the miraculous."[5] More recently, the British biologist Richard Dawkins has claimed that the universe we observe, one ruled by materialist evolution, "has precisely the properties we should expect if there is, at bottom, no design, no purpose, no evil and no good, nothing but blind, pitiless indifference."[6] The philosopher Daniel Dennett, the biologist and historian of science William Provine, and many others have made similar statements.[7] Nor does the challenge presented by Darwinian theory confront Christianity alone, for almost all religious traditions see the cosmos as the expression of a transcendent order, whereas evolution seems to proceed in a random and even pitiless way. Before turning to consider ways in which this challenge may be met, a brief overview of Darwin's theory of evolution by means of natural selection is in order.

The Theory of Evolution by Natural Selection

Historians of science regularly note that the concept of evolution was already being proposed before Charles Darwin was born. His grandfather, Erasmus Darwin, had himself proposed the notion in several of his books, such as *Zoonomia* (1795) and *The Temple of Nature* (1803). Across the English Channel, and likewise near the beginning of the nineteenth century, the French naturalist Jean-Baptiste Lamarck proposed a theory of evolution based on two central ideas: that there is in nature an innate tendency to evolve in increasingly complex ways and that the acquired characteristics of organisms will be passed on to their offspring.[8] However, neither Lamarck's theory nor that of any other naturalist prior to Charles Darwin proved convincing to most scientists.

Darwin's own theory developed slowly, based as it was on a number of interlocking factors, including observations he made during his voyage on *H.M.S. Beagle* during the years 1831–36, studies conducted by some of his scientist friends back in England on the specimens he had collected during the voyage, his reading of Thomas Malthus's *Essay on Population*, and presumed parallels between the "artificial selection" practiced by farmers and breeders as they tried to improve their crops and livestock

of a handful of such catastrophes that occurred during the planet's prehistory.[13]

As noted earlier, the extinction of the dinosaurs provided an opening for the expansion of the class of mammals. More generally, evolutionary theorists hold that after the chance occurrence of a decimation or mass extinction, "there follows a period of rapid diversification and 'experimentation,' which is then greatly reduced by the time half of a given time period has gone by."[14] The important point for our present purposes is that evolutionary theorists see this entire process as strongly influenced by random factors. One such theorist, reflecting a broad consensus among scientists, has written that "there can be little doubt that if the process of evolution on earth would start again from where it was three billion years ago, the evolved organisms would be conspicuously different from the ones that have come about in the first run of the process."[15] Among other things, this means that the appearance of our own species, *Homo sapiens,* should not be thought of as inevitable, though one might still argue that the eventual emergence of some kind of intelligent life would have been likely. It is clear that this kind of conclusion, even though supported by many scientists and theologians, does pose a challenge for traditional understandings of divine providence and of humanity as a race foreordained by God. As will be seen in the following section, there have been several major ways of responding to this and other challenges that the theory of evolution has raised for traditional philosophical and theological thought.

Meeting the Challenges of Evolutionary Theory

One obvious option is to deny the very reality of evolution. Some opponents of the theory base their arguments primarily on religious scriptures such as the opening chapters of the Book of Genesis, understanding the text literally as implying the separate divine creation of individual species. It is easy for those who have been well educated in the natural sciences simply to ignore this kind of opposition, but it must be admitted not only that many persons do stake their claim on the Bible in this way but also that they do so with complete conviction. One of the best refutations of this kind of "scientific creationism" is Kenneth Miller's book *Finding Darwin's God*,[16] but his rebuttals are marked by genuine respect for those with whom he disagrees. One of the most poignant parts of the book describes a breakfast meeting he once had with Henry Morris the day after Miller had forcefully rebutted Morris's creationist position in an academic debate. Miller rather expected that in their private conversation during breakfast Morris would admit that he did not really believe that the earth is relatively young and was only taking this position because it enabled him to earn a comfortable living by representing what millions of Americans actually believe. Miller reports that he was taken aback by Morris's reply to the suggestion that he was not sincere in what he advocated: "Ken, you're intelligent, you're well-meaning, and you're energetic. But you are also young, and you don't realize what's at stake. In a question of such importance, scientific data aren't the ultimate authority. Even you know that science is wrong sometimes."[17] Such a reply indicates that it is not likely that many disciples of Morris in the creationist movement will ever be swayed by scientific arguments of the sort that Miller properly advances in his book.

Another option is to accept the fact of evolution but to reject — in whole or in part — the Darwinian or neo-Darwinian explanation of how it occurred. This option is taken by proponents of "intelligent design," often referred to simply as "ID." One contemporary advocate of this position is the biologist Michael Behe, author of *Darwin's Black Box*.[18] Although Behe frames his argument mostly in terms of biochemistry, he is clearly in the tradition of the nineteenth-century theologian William Paley. One of the latter's best-known books was his *Natural Theology* (1802), which Darwin had read with great admiration while a student at Cambridge and about which something should be said before we turn to Behe's own work. One often finds references to Paley's supposition that if someone were to find a watch while crossing a heath, the person would quickly see that its parts were put together for a purpose and therefore conclude to the existence of a watchmaker. In proceeding to argue for the existence of God, Paley devotes several pages to a detailed account of the working of the human eye. He notes, among other things, the way in which the pupil dilates or contracts so as to admit an appropriate amount of light, all the while retaining its exact circular shape. To perceive objects lying near at hand, a number of other changes must occur simultaneously: the cornea becomes more round and prominent; the crystalline lens underneath the cornea is pushed forward; and the axis of vision (the depth of the eye) is elongated. Just as remarkable is the case of viewing objects in the distance, for a landscape of several square miles is thereby brought into a space merely a half inch in diameter, "yet the multitude of objects which it contains are all preserved, are all discriminated in their magnitudes, positions, figures, colours.... If anything can abate our admiration of the smallness of the visual tablet compared with the extent of vision, it is a reflection...that in the hands of the Creator, great and little are nothing."[19] This last phrase contains the first reference to a Creator in the opening chapters of the book. Even though not put into the form of a syllogism, the nature of Paley's argument for God's existence is clear enough: just as the workmanship of a watch allows one to conclude to the existence of a watchmaker, so does the complex interaction of the parts of the eye point to a still more skillful Maker. If it should be asked, "Why should not the Deity have given to the animal the faculty of vision *at once* ? Why this circuitous perception; the ministry of so many means?" Paley replies that it is only by the display of such "contrivance" that "the existence, the agency, the wisdom of the Deity, *could* be testified to his rational creatures. This is the scale by which we ascend to all the knowledge of our Creator which we possess, so far as it depends upon the phaenomena, or the works of nature."[20]

As noted above, Darwin himself was very impressed by Paley's book during his student days and only gradually came to the conviction that over a very long period of time there could very well have been a progression from the primitive light-sensing properties of bacteria through many intermediate stages up to the remarkable abilities of the eyes of humans and other mammals. Most scientists now hold that Paley's argument from design is not tenable, but there is no absolute unanimity on this point. Michael Behe frequently quotes from the Anglican theologian to bolster his own case, which, as noted above, relies primarily on data from the field of biochemistry. Just as Paley emphasized the great complexity of the human eye, Behe points to "irreducible complexity" in other aspects of living beings (especially in molecular structures) and argues that the degree of complexity is such that it could not have come about by the numerous small modifications that characterize Darwin's theory of natural selection. Rebutting this contention, Kenneth Miller has pointed to a number of studies showing that complex biochemical systems could indeed be produced in a step-by-step Darwinian way. One recent study focused on the Krebs cycle, a very complex series of reactions that release chemical energy from food. The researchers showed that each intermediate stage in the cycle could well be understood as favored by natural selection, the various parts of the cycle being adapted first to different biochemical functions and then modified so as to produce the best chemically possible design.[21]

Probably the greatest weakness in Behe's approach, however, is not that other scientists have come up with findings that he thought highly unlikely (if not impossible) but rather that his own scenario is so implausible. Behe offers the supposition that some four billion years ago "the designer made the first cell, already containing all of the irreducibly complex biochemical systems discussed here and many others. (One can postulate that the designs for systems that were to be used later, such as blood clotting, were present but not 'turned on....')"[22] Miller notes that this means that four billion years ago a simple bacterium would have had to bear "more than a thousand times the genetic information of one of today's bacteria which, strangely, bear no trace of the genes that once were 'present,' waiting to be 'turned on' in the distant future."[23] Moreover, because all those genes were "turned off," not expressed, "natural selection would not be able to weed out genetic mistakes"; mutations would accumulate in these genes in such numbers as to render them "hopelessly changed and inoperative hundreds of millions of years before Behe says that they will be needed."[24] A person surely does not need to be a professional scientist to understand that at least this particular approach to intelligent design is most unconvincing.

Another proponent of intelligent design is William Dembski, who co-authored a book on intelligent design with Behe after having published a book by himself on the same general topic.[25] A subsequent article published on-line succinctly clarifies what he and his colleagues basically reject in Darwinian theory. After affirming that the position of intelligent design is fully compatible with large-scale evolution over the course of natural history (that is, the "full genealogical interconnectedness of all organisms"), he goes on to assert that there is nevertheless no possible compatibility with "the Darwinian mechanism." Darwinism, he writes, must not be identified simply with evolution understood as common descent, for it joins to this historical claim "a naturalistic mechanism," namely, "natural selection operating on random variations," and this mechanism "cannot bear the weight of common descent." Instead, Dembski opts for the possibility that such descent is "driven by telic [or "teleological"] processes inherent in nature (and thus by a form of design)." He admits that it is not easy to "tease apart the effects of intelligent and natural causation" but is quite willing to forgo any claims to an "immediate and easy answer to the question of common descent."[26]

Although I myself am no more convinced by Dembski's specific arguments for intelligent design than I am by Behe's, there is something very significant and enlightening about the points he makes in the article referred to above. Implicit in his critique of the Darwinian "naturalistic mechanism" is a distinction among levels of explanation. From the perspective of and on the level of the life sciences, the kind of work that has gone on since the time of Darwin and under his inspiration can, in my opinion, be heartily affirmed. There are, to be sure, vigorous debates going on among biologists concerning how much relative weight should be given to factors like natural selection, genetic drift, the self-organizing properties of natural arrays, sudden mass extinctions, and so forth. There is no reason to expect such debates to subside in the foreseeable future, though one may hope that continued research and general open-mindedness on the part of the scientists concerned will lead asymptotically to some consensus. Someone who is satisfied simply with a naturalistic explanation of the phenomena of evolution will neither expect nor desire anything more. This is why the atheistic biologist Richard Dawkins says that he cannot understand why any of his fellow scientists spend time reflecting on religious or theological issues raised by modern science.[27] From his perspective, this kind of expenditure of time and energy just does not make sense. However, it is altogether possible to argue that the Darwinian (or neo-Darwinian) theory of evolution is not fully explanatory. Why do elements coalesce, often in terms of greater and greater complexity? Why is nature able to evolve in an apparently self-creative way? May there not be an ultimate "point" or meaning to what some call "the universe story," even if that meaning *could not* show up unambiguously at the level of scientific investigation? These questions are simply not answerable in terms of physics, biology, or other natural sciences and so may properly be called "*meta*physical" or "theological." Pope John Paul II, himself a professionally trained philosopher, pointed to this kind of distinction in an address he made to the Pontifical Academy of Sciences on 22 October 1996, when he said:

> The sciences of observation describe and measure the multiple manifestations of life with increasing precision. . . . The moment of transition to the spiritual cannot be the object of this kind of observation, which nevertheless can discover at the experimental level a series of very valuable signs indicating what is specific to the human being. But the experience of metaphysical knowledge, of self-awareness and self-reflection, of moral conscience, freedom, or . . . aesthetic and religious experience falls within the competence of philosophical analysis and reflection, while theology brings out its ultimate meaning according to the Creator's plans.[28]

Scientists like Behe and philosophers like Dembski understandably are seeking these kinds of "very valuable signs" at the experimental level, but there is an alternative approach that I find much more satisfactory, not least because it is more respectful of different levels of reflection and knowledge. One way of alluding to the difference appeared in theologian John Haught's response to a review of his book *God After Darwin*.[29] The reviewer was Behe himself, who claimed that Haught was in fact falling in line with those who advocate intelligent design. Haught firmly disagreed. While affirming that God is the ultimate source of whatever order emerges in nature, he objected to "the narrowness of any theological approach that seeks to defend the idea of God . . . by focusing exclusively on 'design. . . . ' Design, as Bergson pointed out long ago, is unrepresentative of what we now know about the strange story of life on this planet. . . . Writing as a theologian, my point is that we should not abstract, and then isolate, the element of order from the often disturbing fact of novelty in actually living phenomena."[30] More than a century earlier, John Henry Newman made a similar point by noting the limitations of any argument from design: "Half the world knows nothing of the argument from design — and when you have got it, you do not prove the moral attributes of God — except very faintly. . . . I believe in design because I believe in God, not in a God because I see design."[31] If one asks the further question of why anyone believes (or does not believe) in an order transcending what is accessible to the methods of the natural sciences, Haught is surely correct in saying that "honesty compels us to acknowledge the inevitably personal, fiduciary, and passionate commitments that underlie all of our knowing, including the alleged 'realism' of modern scientific materialism."[32] These personal commitments are, of course, influenced by one's cultural heritage and community belief(s) and are generally more dependent on them than on severely logical arguments. How, then, might one who believes in the reality of God as the ultimate source of all that is but who is simultaneously not convinced by arguments about intelligent design respond to the challenge of evolutionary theory, above all to the central role given to chance in this theory?

In other words, what alternative may there be between agnosticism or atheism on the one hand and intelligent design on the other?

A basic parting of the ways with agnostic or atheistic theorists often occurs with respect to the question of whether there is any underlying directionality in evolution, specifically whether there is any marked tendency toward complexity. Modern Darwinians are often reluctant to admit that anything like phylogenetic complexification even exists and sometimes point out the many species that have in fact evolved into less complex forms. Nevertheless, historians of the evolutionary movement have observed that "even Darwinians are once again flirting with evolutionary direction and complexification."[33] Theistic evolutionists of various persuasions are especially insistent on this point. Paul Davies contends that the general trend of "matter" leading to "mind" and the latter leading to "culture" is a progression "written into the laws of nature at a fundamental level," while John Haught writes that "in view of the discoveries of sciences ranging from astrophysics to biology, today there can be no serious doubt that the natural world has journeyed directionally from simplicity to complexity, from triviality to more intense harmonies of contrast...."[34] Haught, Karl Schmitz-Moormann, Denis Edwards, and other theologians do not, however, understand this directionality in terms of design but rather in light of their understanding of love and of God as a God of love. The basic argument could be developed theologically in several steps.

First of all, granting important differences in nuance, all of the world's major theistic religions regularly speak of God in terms of love and compassion. In the *Bhagavad Gita,* Lord Krishna reveals himself to Arjuna as not only "the goal of life, the Lord and support of all" but also "the only refuge, the one true friend" (9:18). In the *Qur'an,* every sura except one begins with a prayer of invocation: "In the name of God, the Merciful, the Compassionate." Although there is, strictly speaking, no creator god in Buddhism, the Buddhas and Bodhisattvas of the Mahayana tradition are marked by their compassion as well as their wisdom, while within the Judeo-Christian tradition the love of God for creatures is especially prominent. The eleventh chapter of the book of the prophet Hosea begins with the words: "When Israel was a child, I loved him, and out of Egypt I called my son. . . . I led them with cords of compassion, with the bands of love, and I became to them as one who eases the yoke on their jaws, and I bent down to them and fed them" (Hos. 11:1, 4). Of this same God, Jesus says in his Last Supper discourse in John's Gospel: "The hour is coming when I shall no longer speak to you in figures but tell you plainly of the Father. In that day you will ask in my name, and I do not say to you that I shall pray to the Father for you, for the Father himself loves you" (Jn. 16:25–27), and the First Letter of John twice states succinctly that "God is love" (1 Jn. 4:8, 16). Christian literature developed this theme in countless ways, including the famous last line of Dante's *Paradiso* with its reference to "the Love that moves the sun and the other stars."

Dante's words are particularly significant for developing the point I wish to make. Love has often been understood primarily as a moral attitude, but in the *Paradiso*'s final line it is clear that divine love is just as much an ontological force, what Karl Schmitz-Moormann once called "the constitutive force in God's life, . . . the driving force of the evolutionary process of progressing union."[35] Love, in other words, is a force that unites. On the human level this may seem obvious: persons are drawn together by love, not in the sense of being coerced but rather as freely responding to the offer and allure of love shown them by another. A central point made by Schmitz-Moormann and other theologians of similar persuasion is that the same force can be understood as effectively at work among *all* elements in the universe. John Haught emphasizes not only the unitive power of God's love but also its non-coercive character: inviting and alluring but never forcing or imposing. In an essay that is a revised version of a chapter in one of his earlier books, Haught writes: "Since divine creative love has the character of letting things be, we should not be too surprised at evolution's strange and erratic pathways. The long struggle of the universe to arrive at life, consciousness and culture is consonant with faith's conviction that love never forces but always allows for the play of freedom, risk and adventure."[36] Or as he writes elsewhere, because God's love is not coercively manipulative, we should expect that "the world would unfold by responding to the divine allurement at its own pace and in its own particular way."[37] One implication of this understanding of divine love is that God is best understood not merely as a "planner" or "designer," with everything turning out in a predictably orderly fashion, but as a source of genuine novelty and what could even be called "creative disorder."

If the universe is understood as responding in some way to the allurement of divine love, then a further implication of this theological approach is that an element of interiority or subjectivity ought not be reserved to humans alone but rather be seen as pervading the entire cosmos. Such a notion may be found in the works of Alfred North Whitehead and Pierre Teilhard de Chardin, both of whose writings have been viewed with more than a little suspicion by scientists or other scholars who are uncomfortable with the impossibility of testing the notion in controlled experiments. Thus, David Depew and Bruce Weber speak of Whitehead's process philosophy as "a novel philosophical theory" that has gained many adherents because it seems, "in the absence of more concrete evidence, to provide wholesale a metaphysical motor" for the truth of its claims, while the same two authors dismiss Teilhard's theories as providing educated Catholics of the 1960s "with the same kind of spiritual balm that similar theories had offered to liberal Protestants, whose spiritual struggles were similar, half a century earlier."[38] It is certainly true that these theories are not amenable to the "more concrete evidence" that might emerge in a biology laboratory, but this is only to say that philosophical or theological thought operates on a different level and with a different methodology from that of the natural sciences. Anyone who is convinced that there is a God actively present within the universe may well regret that much of modern philosophy and theology, in an apparent effort to "keep up with the times," has "embraced a cosmic picture from which nature's 'subjective' capacity to receive God's influence has already been erased."[39] The alternative, which certainly has the great advantage of providing a more unified view of natural reality and of avoiding the problem of trying to understand how mind or mentality could abruptly arise from its polar opposite, is to affirm that throughout nature there is some capacity to "experience," even if the earliest forms of this capacity ought not be called "conscious." Accordingly, the Australian ecologist Charles Birch has suggested that "some kind of appetition of the individual, freely chosen toward further possibilities, ... must belong to the individual entities of the world."[40] Similarly, Ian Barbour notes that "the approach and avoidance reactions of bacteria can be considered elementary forms of perception and response. An amoeba learns to find sugar, indicating a rudimentary memory and intentionality. ... I would argue that in the light of evolutionary continuity and in the interest of metaphysical generality we should take *experience* as a category applicable to all integrated entities."[41]

Barbour's references to "evolutionary continuity" and "metaphysical generality" are pertinent, for an acceptance of what could be called "pan-experientialism" offers a coherent, integrated understanding of the whole sweep of evolution. On this view, one would not necessarily expect the vast majority of the simplest entities to coalesce and evolve. Schmitz-Moormann writes: "The lower the elements are situated on the scale of becoming, the less they are open to the future. Only a very few hydrogen atoms will ever enter into combination with other elements or will evolve into higher atoms."[42] The transition to life itself will be gradual and in some respects ambiguous. There are various criteria for deciding what is living, such as nutrition, growth, respiration, excretion, responsiveness, and reproduction. How to categorize something as simple as a virus is genuinely problematic, for viruses seem to represent a transitional stage between the non-living and the living.[43] More complex, and clearly alive, are the bacteria, which are sometimes said to be the most successful living entities on earth — far more numerous than other organisms and, in the words of Stephen Jay Gould, "adaptable, indestructible, and astoundingly diverse."[44] As noted earlier, recent discoveries about the human genome provide very strong evidence that all other living beings on earth gradually evolved from bacteria. That bacteria remain far more numerous than other forms of living beings, and that more complex forms of life evolved from them in ways that were dependent on many chance factors (including random genetic mutations and chance collisions of extra-terrestrial objects with the earth, as mentioned earlier in this chapter) should not be regarded as problematic facts for persons of religious faith. Our human line of descent need not be viewed as having occurred inevitably, nor should we assume that everything in the past fifteen billion years of the universe's existence was narrowly directed to the emergence of *Homo sapiens*. As Haught writes, "a robust creation faith demands that we rejoice in the prospect that other natural beings have a meaning and value to their creator that may be quite hidden from our human powers of discernment."[45] The apparent lack of strict order in "the universe story," the fact that some creatures (such as sharks) seem to have changed very little over millions of years while other species rather quickly died out and still others changed markedly, could be viewed as mirroring what we likewise see among the members of the human race. At birth, most infants appear to be very similar, and yet the diversity that marks their adulthood is striking. Why is it that among billions of human beings there so rarely arises a Gandhi, a Churchill, a Mother Teresa? There can never be a completely satisfying answer to such a question, just as there can never be a fully satisfactory explanation for the vast and diversified panorama of life on earth, with many creatures remaining at a quite simple level and others manifesting a marked degree of complexity. A classical theological answer might be that this is just the way a providential God planned it, but there is another understanding of providence that takes more seriously the reality of chance in the saga of evolution. This is the topic to be addressed in the final section of this chapter.

Divine Providence in an Evolutionary World

The term "providence" is not itself biblical, but the notion of a wise and loving God who is in some way guiding the course of world events and of the entire universe is prominent in the Judeo-Christian scriptures. The liberation of the Israelites from Egypt is constantly described as an act of God leading the people to the Promised Land, just as in the New Testament the saving work of Christ and God's predestination of Christ's followers to salvation is described as a divine choice made "before the foundation of the world" (Eph. 1:4). When later theologians worked out a more systematic understanding of divine providence, they strongly affirmed its universal character. Thomas Aquinas, for example, taught that everything is subject to the providence of God. If certain events appear to occur by chance, this can be explained on the basis of a distinction between "a particular cause" (*causa particularis*) and "a universal cause" (*causa universalis*). Aquinas gives the following example to illustrate his point:

> The universal cause is one thing, a particular cause another. An effect can be haphazard with respect to the plan of the second, but not of the first. . . . When an effect escapes from a system of particular causality, we speak of it as a fortuitous or a chance happening, but this is with reference to a particular cause; it cannot stray outside the sway of the universal cause, and with reference to this we speak of it as foreseen. Thus the meeting of two servants, in their eyes unexpected because neither knew the other's errand, was foreseen by their master who intentionally sent them where their paths would cross.[46]

The role that Aquinas gives to chance in his understanding of the relationship between God and creation has been used by some recent theologians to show how God's providential activity can be affirmed even though modern science has emphasized chance to a far greater degree than was the case in earlier times. On the basis of Aquinas's distinction between different levels of causality, Elizabeth Johnson writes that "God works not only through the deep regularities of the laws of nature but also through chance occurrence. . . . God uses chance, so to speak, to ensure variety, resilience, novelty, and freedom in the universe, right up to humanity itself."[47] One could, however, argue that the Thomistic approach does not go far enough. His example of the two servants who *think* they are meeting by chance when in fact their master has planned their meeting all along implies that what appears to be chance is not really so. Detailed planning is at work "behind the scenes." An understanding of divine providence based on this kind of distinction does indeed have a venerable history, but current thinking about the full implications of God's love points to the need for some modification of this idea of providence. If love at its best is non-coercive, then it could well be understood as allowing creatures to evolve in novel ways that would better not be described as "divinely foreseen." On this point, John Haught writes: "Since divine creative love has the character of letting things be, we should not be too surprised at evolution's strange and erratic pathways. The long struggle of the universe to arrive at life, consciousness, and culture is consonant with faith's conviction that love never forces but always allows for the play of freedom, risk and adventure."[48]

This does not mean that there are no boundaries to "evolution's strange and erratic pathways." In speaking of God's relationship to the world we necessarily use analogies drawn from our own experience and these may not be altogether adequate, but one that seems promising concerns the game of chess. The final outcome of the game depends on free choices as the players make their moves, but these are always made within the general framework of the rules of the game. Certain pieces are allowed to move only in certain ways. It is this combination of law-like framework and free moves within the framework that gives such a game its perennial appeal. So too, though in ways that we could never expect to comprehend fully, it is theologically arguable that God's creation is itself set within a framework exhibiting a considerable degree of order, but not to the extent of preventing genuine creativity and novelty on the part of elements that make up the natural world.[49] This is why Darwin, even though not writing as a professedly religious man, was in fact a better theologian than his fundamentalist opponents when he penned the final lines of *On the Origin of Species,* lines that bear repeating as this chapter comes to an end:

"There is grandeur in this view of life, with its several powers having been originally breathed by the Creator into a few forms or into one; and that, whilst this planet has gone cycling on according to the fixed law of gravity, from so simple a beginning endless forms most wonderful and most beautiful have been, and are being evolved."

4

Evolution and the
Doctrine of the Human Soul

A KEY DISTINCTION underlying the various arguments in this book is that there are different branches of knowledge, each with its own area of competency. As noted in the previous chapter, Pope John Paul II's 1996 address to the Pontifical Academy of Sciences pointed out that "the sciences of observation" have been studying various manifestations of life with increasing precision but are methodologically unable to deal with the kinds of questions that fall within the province of philosophical and/or theological analysis. Accordingly, those who maintain that philosophy and theology simply cannot offer convincing reasons for maintaining that there is, for example, an ultimate point to the universe will necessarily opt for ultimate meaninglessness, however satisfying may be the islands of meaning they construct for themselves.[1] On the other hand, those who agree that there is a valid role for philosophy and theology will not necessarily be unanimous in their particular conclusions, as even a cursory survey of the history of these disciplines would show. A pertinent example of diversity arises from the specific issue that the pope was addressing on the occasion of his address in 1996. After affirming that evolution ought to be recognized as a theory and not merely an hypothesis, he went on to say that in fact there is not simply one theory of evolution but several, not all of which are compatible with Christian faith. After referring to Pope Pius XII's 1950 encyclical *Humani Generis*, which spoke of evolution as a serious hypothesis, worthy of investigation provided that this did not entail a denial that human souls are directly created by God, John Paul II reiterated this condition: "If the human body takes its origin from pre-existent living matter, the spiritual soul is immediately created by God."[2] Strictly materialistic understandings of evolution, according to which the human soul would be regarded as non-existent or as a mere epiphenomenon of living matter, were rejected by the pope as incompatible with the truth about the human person. There is, however, diversity among those who join him in rejecting the materialistic position, for some theologians are seeking an alternative to the doctrine of a directly created soul that lives on as a separate entity (*anima separata*) in an "intermediate" (or "interim") state after a person dies. Why this search, and how successful might it be? These are among the main questions to be considered in this chapter.

Different Understandings of the Soul in the Light of Evolution

Many persons reading about the direct creation of a self-subsistent soul by God will have no difficulty at all accepting this doctrine literally, since it seems so entirely consistent with a perceived difference between human beings and all other forms of life. One certainly need not be a religious believer to hold that there is a sharp difference. The American biologist George Gaylord Simpson, who was quoted in the previous chapter praising Darwin for destroying "the last stronghold of the supernatural, the providential and the miraculous," nevertheless considered humans to be qualitatively different from all other animals. He wrote: "Man has certain diagnostic features which set him off most sharply from any other animal and which have involved other developments not only increasing this sharp distinction but also making it an absolute difference in kind and not only a relative difference of degree."[3] Other authors, however, have placed more emphasis on continuity between humans and other species. As Aristotle once observed:

In the great majority of animals there are traces of psychical qualities or attitudes, which qualities are more markedly differentiated in the case of human beings. For just as we pointed out resemblances in the physical organs, so in a number of animals we observe gentleness or fierceness, mildness or cross temper, courage or timidity, fear or confidence, high spirit or low cunning, and, with regard to intelligence, something equivalent to sagacity. Some of these qualities in man, as compared with the corresponding qualities in animals, differ only quantitatively . . . ; other qualities in man are represented by analogous and not identical qualities: for instance, just as in man we find knowledge, wisdom, and sagacity, so in certain animals there exists some other natural potentiality akin to these.[4]

Even though Aristotle clearly affirms differences, his emphasis here is on similarity and continuity, and various scholars have made this point even more forcefully since the time of Darwin. Among these is Jane Goodall, perhaps the best-known and most-respected primatologist of our time. Reminiscing on the forty years she has spent observing chimpanzees, she recently wrote:

Chimpanzees are capable of intellectual skills once thought unique to our own species — such as abstraction, generalization, use and understanding of abstract symbols in communication, understanding the wants and moods of others, and the ability to plan ahead. They have prodigious memories. They show care and concern for each other, which can result in true altruism. They grieve the death of a family member. They have a sense of self and a sense of humor. We know too that they experience and express emotions similar to those we label sadness, joy, fear, despair, and anger, among others. This teaches us we humans are not as different from the rest of the animal kingdom as we once thought.[5]

Pope John Paul II alluded to this kind of continuity in his above-mentioned address, for after affirming "an ontological difference, an ontological leap, one could say," between humans and other animals, he went on to ask: "However, does not the posing of such ontological discontinuity run counter to that physical continuity which seems to be the main thread of research into evolution in the field of physics and chemistry?"[6] The continuity is striking enough that those who affirm a direct creation of a soul at or near the time of conception of each human being would surely find it impossible to say just when this first occurred: With *Homo habilis* some two and a half million years ago? With *Homo erectus* approximately 500,000 years later? Did *Homo sapiens neanderthalensis* have a soul directly created by God? The British theologian Paul Badham expresses the difficulty in the following way: "Taking evolution as a whole, it seems impossible to make sense of the claim that at some point in the process one of our hominid ancestors acquired an immortal soul and thus became a full human being. There simply is no sharp intelligible dividing line."[7] Even if one should posit such a dividing line at which the first immortal soul was created, one would still face the question of whether the "human" qualities of this new being were so different from those of creatures just antecedent that one could in no sense speak of a soul for the latter. And if one should choose to use "soul" language even for earlier forms of life, would one still claim that only human souls are directly and divinely created, while all others somehow arise in a non-supernatural way?

In the light of such questions, it is not surprising that contemporary thinkers take a wide variety of positions on the matter of the human soul. At one end of the spectrum are those who simply avoid the question of the existence of the soul, not merely because its existence is not scientifically provable but because the very concept appears superfluous and hence unhelpful. Reviewing a book with the provocative title *Whatever Happened to the Soul?* theologian Michael Barnes notes: "The chapters by scientists, in biology and psychology, provide the background for understanding why a body-soul dualism looks increasingly implausible to account for cognition and choice, and how self-reflective awareness could emerge from the evolutionary history of interpersonal and linguistic relations." Without taking a firm position himself, Barnes does suggest that "if various fields in modern science are rendering the idea of a spiritual soul implausible or at least unnecessary, Christianity must be willing to take this into account."[8] Similarly the philosopher Klaus Kremer, himself a proponent of the reality of the soul, writes that "modern science often considers the notion of the soul as a separate reality to be not only superfluous but even untenable and therefore non-existent."[9] This position has been aggressively advocated by the philosopher Daniel Dennett, who bluntly asserts that "there is only one sort of stuff, namely matter."[10]

One contemporary approach that avoids Dennett's materialism on the one hand and strict dualism on the other is called "dual-aspect monism" or "non-reductive physicalism." A prominent representative of this position is John Polkinghorne, who taught mathematical physics at Cambridge University for many years before retiring to study theology and be ordained an Anglican priest. Explicitly noting both the continuity that seems to mark the story of evolution and the close relationship between body and mind evident in the practice of modern medicine, he eschews the traditional dualism that viewed the soul as a separate entity. For him, "knowledge of the effects of drugs and brain damage on mental behavior, together with consideration of the long evolutionary history that links human beings to animals and ultimately to inanimate matter in early Earth, encourage an altogether more integrated, psychosomatic understanding of human nature, of a kind at least as old as the writers of the Hebrew Bible." For this reason, he espouses "dual-aspect monism, a complementary relationship of mind and matter as contrasting poles of the process and organization of the one stuff of the created world."[11]

Of the same overall persuasion are the contributors to the above-mentioned book *Whatever Happened to the Soul?* Preferring the terminology of "non-reductive physicalism" to that of "dual-aspect monism," the contributors to this volume include a geneticist, a biologist, three psychologists, a biomedical ethicist, a philosopher, a theologian, and a biblical exegete. On the one hand, the authors clearly distance themselves from the reductive materialism of someone like Dennett, who claims that "the mind is somehow nothing but a physical phenomenon. In short, the mind is the brain."[12] Hence their emphasis on the adjective "nonreductive," as when psychologist Malcolm Jeeves writes that "we regard mental activity as *embodied in* brain activity rather than as being *identical with* brain activity. To go beyond that and to adopt what is sometimes called the materialist view is to confuse categories that belong to different logical levels."[13] On the other hand, the contributors to this volume consider the traditional dualistic approach to be based on a misunderstanding. Nancey Murphy argues: "We have been misled by the fact that 'mind' and 'soul' are nouns into thinking that there must be an object to which these terms correspond. Rather, we say that a person is intelligent, and by this we mean that the person behaves or has the disposition to behave in certain ways; we do not mean to postulate the existence of a substance, intelligence. . . . [So too] with regard to the soul."[14] Writing several decades before Jeeves, Murphy, and their colleagues, the Dutch philosopher C. A. van Peursen made a similar point when he said that "the terms 'soul' and 'body' are being wrested from their use in everyday speech and misapplied, philosophically speaking, if taken to refer to certain self-subsistent substances. If we do so understand them, we force soul and body apart in an arbitrary way, and the final result is to isolate the whole man from his world."[15]

There are, of course, numerous scholars who strongly affirm the reality of the soul as a substance distinct from the body. The next section of this chapter will examine some of the main sources of this tradition, but this has certainly been for centuries a prominent position within Christianity. One of its strongest advocates today is Cardinal Joseph Ratzinger, who published extensively on the subject while still a theology professor before being named prefect of the Congregation for the Doctrine of the Faith at the Vatican. Writing as a theologian but noting that scientists like the neurophysiologist John Eccles and philosophers like Karl Popper likewise affirm a certain kind of dualism,[16] Ratzinger emphasizes the Christian conviction that those who have died in Christ are in fact alive. This conviction is evident at a number of places in the New Testament, including the dialogue between Jesus on the cross and the good thief, who receives the promise, "Today you will be with me in Paradise" (Lk. 23:43). Ratzinger affirms the way Joachim Jeremias pointed to a connection between the good thief's prayer to be remembered by Jesus and the petition of the first Christian martyr, Stephen, who prayed: "Lord Jesus, receive my spirit" (Acts 7:59). In the words of Jeremias, "with impressive unanimity... the New Testament presents communion with Christ after death as the specifically Christian view of the intermediate state."[17] Against authors who avoid affirming the reality of a spiritual soul that survives death, Ratzinger argues that the Christian conviction that one is called to be "with Christ" after death means "the continuing authentic reality of the person in separation from his or her body."[18] This is what the very notion of the soul is intended to convey: According to Christian faith, a human being can "live forever, because he is able to have a relationship with that which gives the eternal. 'The soul' is our term for that in us which offers a foothold for this relation. Soul is nothing other than man's capacity for relatedness with truth, with love eternal."[19]

In light of the various positions briefly described above — reductive materialism (Dennett), dual-aspect monism (Polkinghorne, Jeeves, and Murphy), and dualism (Ratzinger, who nevertheless does not deny a body-soul unity inasmuch as the soul desires reunion with the body in what the Christian creeds call "the resurrection of the body" at the end of time) — it is obvious that the subject matter of this chapter gives rise to numerous questions. Some of these have been noted by the British biochemist M. J. C. Crabbe in the following words: "Do we have souls? Are souls sources of life or of mind? If souls exist, are they material or immortal? Can the soul be distinguished from the self? What criteria do we use for individual identity? Can animal souls be distinguished from human souls?"[20] As an aid toward answering some of these questions, the next section of this chapter will look briefly at some of the beliefs about the soul that lie behind the position advocated by a theologian like Joseph Ratzinger. A still later section will examine an alternative to this position.

Some Classic Understandings of the Soul in the Western World

Examining all the ways in which human beings have understood themselves would be the work of more than one lifetime. Even if one limited oneself to the field of philosophy, one would come up against what Richard Sorabji has called "the enormous variety of concepts of the self in ancient philosophy, and of contexts for discussing the self.... I believe this variety defies any attempt to find a single dominant conception, or a single mistake that makes all the conceptions chimerical."[21] Many persons in the modern West have been intrigued by the question of the soul-body or mind-body relationship, but this has not been a major issue for all peoples. In a telling incident, the anthropologist Maurice Leenhardt once asked an elderly Pacific islander whether it was not the notion of "spirit" that the West had brought to his people. No, came the reply: "We already knew about that — but what you have given us is the notion of the body."[22] In other words, prior to the arrival of the Western anthropologists and missionaries, "the 'I' was not yet delimited or defined and could quite well be located 'out there', say, in a tree. Now, however, the old man says 'I'. He is the self who activates his body."[23]

If there was this much difference in self-understanding between Pacific islanders and their early Western visitors, there was also much diversity within the archaic West. One sometimes hears of sharp dichotomies between a monolithic dualistic Greek way of thinking about the human person and a more integral view found within Hebrew thought. Whatever basis there may be for a distinction of this sort, more careful consideration shows it to be too sweeping a generalization. At the beginning of Greek literature, the two Homeric epics speak of an abode of souls, the shadowy realm of Hades visited by the slain suitors of Penelope when they were led there by the god Hermes:

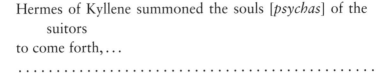

Hermes of Kyllene summoned the souls [*psychas*] of the
    suitors
to come forth, . . .
. . . .
They went along, and passed the Ocean stream, and the
    White Rock,
and passed the gates of Helios the sun, and the country
of dreams, and presently arrived in the meadow of asphodel.
This is the dwelling place of souls, images of dead men.
    There they found the soul of Achilleus, the son of Peleus,
the soul of Patroklos, and the soul of stately Antilochos,
and the soul of Aias, who for beauty and stature was greatest
of all the Danaans, next to the blameless son of Peleus.
So these were gathered around Achilleus, and now came to
    them
the soul of Agamemnon, the son of Atreus, sorrowing,
and around him were gathered the souls of those others,
    who with him
also died and met their fate in the house of Aigisthos.[24]

In this passage, "soul" does not refer to an entity distinct from
the body but rather to the entire person in a state of vital dimin-
ishment. The shadowy nature of this underworld is reminiscent of
some of the passages in the Hebrew Bible, as when the witch of
Endor conjures up the spirit of the dead Samuel to confront King
Saul (1 Sam. 28) — Greek Hades and Hebrew Sheol are somewhat kindred realms, each inhabited by the shades of persons who
once lived on earth.[25] This alone is enough to give one pause before making too sharp a distinction between Greek and Hebrew
thought concerning an element or aspect of the human person
that continues to exist in some way after death. In addition, there
was considerable diversity about the nature of the soul *within* the
Greek tradition and even within the writings of individual Greek
thinkers. In the *Phaedo* Plato has Socrates speak of the body as a
kind of prison for the soul, so that "as long as we are alive, we
shall continue closest to knowledge if we avoid as much as we

can all contact and association with the body, except when this is absolutely necessary, and instead of allowing ourselves to become infected with its nature, purify ourselves from it until God himself gives us deliverance."[26] There is no doubt but that this sharp dualism influenced certain major strains of subsequent Christian thought, but Plato himself takes a less negative view of the body in some of his later treatises,[27] while his disciple Aristotle advocated an integral connection between soul and body.

The Aristotelian notion of the soul as the form of the body became influential within Christianity only in the thirteenth century, largely through the extensive use that Thomas Aquinas made of Aristotle's philosophy, but the appropriation was marked by significant changes. For Aristotle, the soul is an "entelechy," an actualization that is so totally dependent on the body (and the body on it) that the two are *one* just as clay is one with the imprint it has received. With the demise of the body, the soul likewise ceases to exist. The only truly spiritual element in the human being according to Aristotle is *nous,* mind, seen not as individual or personal but as a human participation in a divine, transcendent principle, an *anima mundi.* Not surprisingly, a Christian theologian like Aquinas could not accept this aspect of Aristotle's teaching about the soul, so he took the momentous step of arguing that the spiritual aspect of the human person is not a universal "soul of the world" but is at one and the same time something personal and also the form of the body. It is, in other words, a *substantial* form. Ratzinger comments: "Compared with all the conceptions of the soul available in antiquity, this notion of the soul is quite novel. It is a product of Christian faith, and of the exigencies of faith for human thought."[28]

This Thomistic understanding of the relationship between soul and body eventually became normative for Roman Catholic theology. It does not ignore the classic Christian belief in the resurrection of the body but understands the substantiality of the soul as allowing one to posit the possibility of truly being "with Christ" even in the intermediate period between one's earthly death and the eventual resurrection. Some Protestant denominations, especially ones of Calvinistic provenance, hold a somewhat similar doctrine. Calvin himself wrote: "It is neither lawful nor expedient to inquire too curiously concerning our soul's intermediate state.... Scripture goes no farther than to say that Christ is present with them, and receives them into paradise (cf. John 12:32) that they may obtain consolation.... Let us be content with the limits divinely set for us: namely, that the souls of the pious, having ended the toil of their warfare, enter into blessed rest, where in glad expectation they await the enjoyment of promised glory, ... "[29]

Whatever difficulties have been raised against the position that the souls of the departed continue in existence, all the while expecting an eventual reunion with their bodies, at the very least it has the advantage of presenting a more unified understanding of the human person than does the sharp dualism formulated by René Descartes three centuries after the time of Aquinas. The French thinker wrote in his *Meditations:* "I am not that structure of limbs which is called a human body. I am not even some thin vapour which permeates the limbs — a wind, fire, air, breath, or whatever I depict in my imagination; for these are things which I have supposed to be nothing. Without changing this supposition, I find that I am still certain that I am something."[30] Descartes gave the name *res cogitans* to this "something" and limited its existence to human beings. Other animals were understood simply as machines, leading him to write: "Doubtless when the swallows come in spring, they operate like clocks. The actions of honey bees are of the same nature, and the discipline of cranes in flight, and of apes in fighting, if it is true that they keep discipline."[31] The many reported accounts of the brutal way in which some Cartesians treated animals can only be understood against the background of this philosophy, which denied that any earthly beings other than humans had souls and thus the ability to feel pain.

While this sharp Cartesian dualism has few adherents today, the modified dualism of Aquinas is widely held in many philosophical and theological circles, especially within Roman Catholicism. Even persons who may never have read Thomistic works represent this position in believing (1) that the human soul is directly created by God at or near the time of each human being's conception and (2) that this soul does not cease existing with the death of the body but is — either at once or after a period of purification from the effects of sin — able to enjoy the heavenly bliss traditionally called "the beatific vision," even though this celestial happiness will be further enhanced when the soul is reunited with its body at the resurrection at the end of time. One finds this traditional teaching clearly enunciated in the official *Catechism of the Catholic Church:* "The Church teaches that every spiritual soul is created immediately by God — it is not 'produced' by the parents — and also that it is immortal: it does not perish when it separates from the body at death, and it will be reunited with the body at the final Resurrection."[32] Nevertheless, there is remarkably little said about this teaching in many theological works of our time. The prominent and theologically moderate *New Dictionary of Theology* does not even have an entry for "Soul" but simply refers the reader to the article on "Christian Anthropology," where in fact the word "soul" does not appear even once in the entry's twenty-seven columns![33] This is but one indication of a general reluctance among many theologians to use the word "soul." This is so much the case that Ratzinger has noted with regret that "even the new Roman Missal suppressed the term *anima* in its liturgy for the dead. It also disappeared from the ritual for burial."[34]

There are surely many reasons for this general disappearance of soul-language from Christian discourse. Within Protestantism, the discomfiture began already with Martin Luther, who wrote that the distinction between soul and body that many people had used in trying to explain the beggar Lazarus's life "in the bosom of Abraham" (Lk. 16:23) was *ein Dreck,* "a load of rubbish." Rather, "we must say *totus Abraham,* the whole man, is to live."[35] A similar uneasiness with this kind of distinction has appeared more recently within Roman Catholic theology, due no doubt in part to a sense that the notion of a self-subsistent soul is non-scriptural and/or that the notion of God's immediately creating each human soul does not fit easily into the continuum of living beings that marks the theory of evolution. We have already seen that Pope

John Paul II alluded to this latter point by saying that the "onto-logical leap" that marks the emergence of human beings with their spiritual souls is something beyond the ken of the observational sciences as such. One may readily grant his point that philosoph-ical and theological issues cannot be adjudicated by the natural sciences and also agree with his evident desire to affirm a tran-scendent dimension to human beings against materialist denials of such a dimension and nevertheless wonder whether there may not be a way of arguing for this transcendence that is more in accord with what he calls the "sciences of observation." The following section, after reviewing some further details about the traditional Catholic doctrine, will consider this possibility.

Toward a Contemporary Understanding of the Soul

When considering the way in which a particular theological doc-trine may be viewed in the light of modern science, two extremes should be avoided, even though the resulting middle ground will itself leave room for various options. On the one hand, it would be rash to hold that the methodological differences between the-ology and natural science are so significant that the former need not be open to any reformulation of its doctrines in order to re-main in better accord with scientific findings. The condemnation of Galileo is a well-known instance of the harm caused by such a position. A more recent example may be found in the fact that the *Catechism of the Catholic Church* continues to teach in an un-nuanced way that if the first human being had not sinned but had "remained in the divine intimacy, man would not have to suffer or die" (No. 376), a position that was held literally by patristic and medieval theologians but is fundamentally at odds with what we have learned from science. As Joan Acker, a religious sister and professor of science, has written, "Microorganisims, preceding hu-mans by 3.6 billion years, make the preternatural gifts taught in the Roman catechism historically impossible. Science reinforces theol-ogy in recognizing that disease and death have always been part of God's plan for earthly becoming."[36] To teach otherwise makes

Christian doctrine appear incredible to educated persons. On the other hand, it is also the case that scientific theories are in principle always open to revision and have in fact often been revised. Theologians should therefore resist the temptation to jettison traditional formulations simply because these seem incompatible with some new scientific theory, for the latter may itself prove to be short-lived. The following reflections on the soul will attempt to avoid these extremes and so arrive at a position that is both faithful to traditional Christian understandings of the human person and consonant with what natural science is telling us about the relationship of human beings to the rest of creation.

To begin, let us recall Joseph Ratzinger's point that, according to Christian faith, a human being can "live forever, because he is able to have a relationship with that which gives the eternal. 'The soul' is our term for that in us which offers a foothold for this relation."[37] The basic question is, then, whether there is some aspect or element of the human person that survives bodily death. While some Christians may naively believe that all religious persons readily give an affirmative answer to this question, this is by no means the case. For many centuries in ancient Israel there was no clear conviction about an afterlife, and yet many of the Israelites of that time were most zealous in their religious dedication to Yahweh their Lord. The Buddhist doctrine of *anatta* (no abiding, substantial self or soul) means that that religion's understanding of *nirvana* bears little or no resemblance to a Christian or Islamic notion of heaven, for there is no self to abide in the nirvanic realm. Even within the various Christian denominations there are major divergences concerning what is often called "the immortality of the soul." We have already seen that Roman Catholicism and some Protestant denominations teach that there is an intermediate state in which the souls of the departed abide while awaiting the resurrection of the body, but other Christian denominations and theologians emphasize only the resurrection "at the end of time" and consider any affirmation of the soul's immortality to be an illicit importation from Greek thought that has no scriptural warrant.[38] Before the end-time there is only the sleep of death rather than any kind of heavenly existence on the part of a self-subsistent soul.

That there should be such divergence among some of the world's religions and even within the Christian religion is not surprising. In dealing with this kind of issue, it is well to keep in mind the need for theological humility. Zachary Hayes, who has published extensively on theological questions dealing with death and afterlife, gives evidence of such humility with his implicit use of a traditional distinction between faith and knowledge when he writes: "Because of the ambiguity of human experience, it is never clear what lies in store for us in or beyond death. Do we finally meet a void of nothingness, or do we meet a mystery of fullness and completion? No one standing on this side of death can claim to know the answer to this."[39] The tentative answer of strict materialists is that every human death means simple and complete personal oblivion for the one who died. On the contrary, the traditional Roman Catholic doctrine is that God directly creates a spiritual soul for each human being at or near the time of conception and that at death this self-subsistent soul enters a state of either everlasting bliss (Heaven), temporary purification (Purgatory), or unending damnation (Hell). A corollary of this doctrine, based primarily on the thought of Thomas Aquinas, is that the self-subsistent nature of the human soul is due to its intellectual or rational nature, which is not dependent on matter for its operation (in contrast to the "sensitive soul" of animals or the "vegetative soul" of plants). The scriptural foundation of this latter distinction is primarily the verse in the opening book of the Bible that refers to human beings as created in the image and likeness of God (Gen. 1:26), the implication being that this is a privilege applicable to humans alone. As noted earlier in this chapter — and as is regularly taught in Catholic catechesis — the soul that exists in the "intermediate state" following death is in an incomplete state, such that it desires reunification with the body at the time of the resurrection. Among classic Christian theologians who have given expression to this longing is St. Bernard of Clairvaux, who writes: "Until death is swallowed up in victory [1 Cor. 15:54] and the everlasting light invades the farthest bounds of night and shines everywhere — so that heavenly glory gleams even in bodies — these souls cannot wholly remove themselves and transport themselves to God. They are still too much bound to their bodies, if not in life and feeling, certainly in natural affection. They do not wish to be complete without them, and indeed they cannot be."[40] Roman Catholic doctrine, as commonly understood, holds that only Jesus and his mother Mary have fully entered heavenly bliss "body and soul," the former through his resurrection, the latter in virtue of her assumption (defined infallibly as Catholic doctrine by Pope Pius XII in 1950). Because saints other than Mary are not yet in heavenly glory in this fullest sense, strict Thomistic doctrine holds that prayers to them are not really addressed to them as persons. The Catholic philosopher Wolfgang Kluxen notes in this connection that since the separated soul is no longer a "person" (which by definition implies a body-soul unity), St. Thomas is consistent in teaching that the souls of the saints that are now enjoying the *visio beatifica* have a "personal" aspect only insofar as these souls were once constitutive of persons on earth and will again be such after the resurrection of the body. "Nevertheless, the soul of St. Peter, to whom the Church prays, is not St. Peter."[41]

Since the liturgy of the Catholic Church does not make this kind of distinction between prayers to Mary and those to other saints (as in the Litany of the Saints), and since most members of the church probably do not make this distinction in their private devotions either,[42] a helpful entrée into the question of the state of those who have died may be found in the church's teaching about Mary. In one of his earliest published articles, the German theologian Karl Rahner asked just what was actually meant by the defined dogma of Mary's assumption into heaven "body and soul." He argues that the fundamental meaning is that "Mary in her entire being is already where perfect redemption exists, entirely in that region of being which came to be through Christ's Resurrection."[43] This "privilege" is unique to her "in virtue of her divine Motherhood and her unique position in saving history," but this does not necessarily mean that the state of being in the fullness of redemption "body and soul," that is, in one's entire being, cannot be affirmed of other holy persons as well. Rahner points to the passage in Matthew's Gospel (27:51–53) that affirms that at the time of Jesus' death the earth shook, the tombs were opened, and "many bodies of the saints who had fallen asleep were raised." To be sure, scripture scholars regularly point out that earthquakes, the opening of tombs, and the raising of the dead are part of the common "furniture" of apocalyptic descriptions of the end-time in intertestamental literature,[44] but both Rahner and some prominent scripture scholars insist that the Matthean text is an integral part of the properly Christian understanding of the definitive, eschatological significance of Jesus' death. In John Meier's words, these signs and wonders worked by God in response to Jesus' death "are not just superficial apocalyptic color" but are "Matthew's way of affirming that, with the death of the Son, a new age has broken into the old," with the dead rising "in a proleptic final resurrection."[45] A seventeenth-century Doctor of the Church, St. Francis de Sales, was writing out of a similar conviction when, in a spiritual conference about St. Joseph, he averred that "this glorious saint has much influence in Heaven with the One [Jesus] who so favored him that he raised him there in body and in soul," for "how could He who had been so obedient to St. Joseph throughout His life refuse him this grace?"[46]

In affirming this, Francis de Sales undoubtedly assumed that the bodily remains of St. Joseph did not in any sense remain on earth, but I am suggesting that the more fundamental truth that Francis and the evangelist Matthew are teaching is that those who have led truly holy lives on earth are even now so fully in God's presence that they can be said to be there "body and soul" even if their corpse rests in a grave. This was one of Rahner's main points when, toward the end of the above-mentioned article, he wrote that Mary's "privilege" does *not* mean that "Mary alone enjoyed it" or that what she experienced was something that in the case of other holy persons "could only 'really' emerge later. On the contrary: salvation has already advanced so far historically that since the Resurrection it is completely 'normal' (which is not to say 'general') that there should be men [and women] in whom sin and death have already been definitively overcome."[47] Christ's entry into eternal glory "institutes a bodily community of the redeemed," however far from complete the number of them may already be. Rahner did not claim that entry into the "bodily community of the redeemed" could be affirmed of everyone who dies, but only that those who are fully in God's presence may truly be said to be there "body and soul," however incapable we are of forming an idea of the new condition of the body in that state of radical transformation that St. Paul referred to with the expression "spiritual body" (*sōma pneumatikon*) (1 Cor. 15:44).[48]

However radical this suggestion may appear from the point of view of classical Catholic theology, it does correlate well with the basic conviction that the saints really are already fully with God. It likewise avoids the need for pointless speculations about how or when billions of bodies of deceased human beings might suddenly be raised up on earth. There was a time when serious consideration was given to determining the precise location where all the bodies of the risen would be gathered at the "general resurrection" (usually in the vicinity of Jerusalem). What we now know of the vast numbers of human beings who have ever lived, and of the possibly billions more who will one day live on earth or even elsewhere in the cosmos, makes such speculation seem absurdly quaint if not absolutely incredible. The avoidance of even the need for such theorizing is surely a major advantage of the line of thinking opened up by Rahner's article on Mary's assumption. What, however, does this approach mean for our understanding of the soul and its relationship with the body?

As an approach to answering this question in a way that is consonant with the main tenets of Christian eschatology, it is helpful to start with the fact that the biblical view of the human person is basically not dualistic. As Ratzinger himself wrote in an early article, "biblical thought presupposes an indivisible unity of man; for example, the Bible has no term which signifies only the body (separated and differentiated from the soul); vice versa, the word 'soul' always means the whole man existing bodily."[49] According to this perspective, which is shared by much contemporary philosophy, body and soul are two *aspects* or elements of *the one* human person, the body being the *expression* of the soul, the human soul being what Ratzinger elsewhere termed our "capacity for relatedness with truth, with love eternal."[50] By not seeing body and soul as two separate entities and accordingly recognizing that an element of bodiliness is an integral aspect of the soul just as an element of interiority is an integral aspect of the body, it becomes possible to argue that at death the soul does not simply abandon this bodily aspect, even though the spatio-temporal conditions characteristic of earthly life then come to an end.

A number of theologians refer to this possibility as "resurrection in death." One of the objections to this understanding comes from Ratzinger. Although he seems to have been favorably disposed toward this notion when he wrote his above-quoted article on resurrection in the late 1960s, he later argued that a typical Christian believer could not possibly believe that a dead friend, whom he has seen buried, has been resurrected. To argue thus, he said, would be to resort to typical academic terminology, *lingua docta,* which simply cannot express a "common and commonly understood faith."[51] This does not seem to be a conclusive objection, however, since in fact some Christians in the early Church did claim in their "common faith" to have seen martyrs not only die but also appear as bodily resurrected.[52] This is not to say that such appearances portrayed the actual nature of a resurrected body, for there seems to be no way for a believer to *know* exactly what the fullness of life with God is like. St. Paul's words about seeing now "in a mirror, dimly" (1 Cor. 13:12) must never be forgotten when one tries to give some expression to this aspect of Christian faith. Nevertheless, the abiding conviction of many believers that the saints are already now fully with God does lend support to the notion of "resurrection in death."

This conviction also correlates well with the overall direction of contemporary philosophy. As Karl Rahner once wrote, "in view of its understanding of the unity of man, modern metaphysical anthropology can never (or only with the greatest reservations) consider that an intermediate state, or an absolutely non-material mode of existence on the part of the spiritual subject, is possible."[53] What Rahner said of metaphysical anthropology could surely be said of the conviction of many persons in general, even ones not philosophically trained. The notion of an absolutely disembodied soul existing in an "intermediate state" until some time in the future when the bodies of all the human beings who ever lived will suddenly be raised up can all too readily seem completely unbelievable. Rahner concludes his article on the intermediate state by saying that "it is impossible to overlook the difficulties many people find in this idea today. For these people it may be a help to say that the idea is not really strictly binding from a theological point of view, and that consequently it is open to the individual believer to follow the theological arguments which he finds convincing."[54] It is not a matter of watering down the faith, which will always pose ineluctable challenges, but of ensuring that what is taught as being necessarily "of faith" is truly so.

Who Are Called to Eternal Life?

One further question remains to be treated in this chapter, one that may well appear more marginal than "resurrection in death" but that nevertheless does arise in light of what evolutionary science claims about continuity between human beings and other forms of life. Thus far we have only considered the question of what it means to say that someone is called to eternal life with God. In traditional Christian theology, such bliss was regularly restricted to humans, since they alone were believed to be made in the image and likeness of God (Gen. 1:26). All other living beings were generally thought simply to fall into nothingness at the time of death. One might nevertheless ask if this is really so. Just as it was asked above if the privilege ascribed to Mary in the Catholic dogma of her assumption into heaven body and soul could not in some sense be attributed to other holy persons as well, so too one might ask if the general human "privilege" of being in the divine image and likeness could not in some degree be attributed to other living beings. If so, might this not open up the possibility of thinking that they too in some way survive earthly life?

I am fully aware that this kind of question may at first sight seem rather fanciful, the kind of question that might concern a child who hopes her deceased pet is "in heaven" but that is irrelevant to mature persons. All the same, some insights into the full meaning of Christian faith may be gleaned from reflecting on this point. A few years ago Elizabeth Johnson, in her presidential address at the annual meeting of the Catholic Theological Society of America, quoted a passage from one of Annie Dillard's best-known books and then reflected on it from a theological point of view. Dillard had written of a small goldfish she had once purchased for twenty-five cents and had named Ellery, a creature with "a coiled gut, a spine radiating fine bones, and a brain. . . . And, he has a heart."[55] What, asked Johnson, would be an appropriate theological interpretation of this creature? Using Aquinas's notion that all creatures exist by participation in divine being, she writes that this suggests "an intrinsic, ongoing relationship with the very wellspring of being, with the sheer livingness of the living God who in overflowing graciousness quickens all things."[56] This in turn gives rise to a number of other questions, including whether "this glorious little fish [is] in some way an image of God."[57] Johnson would answer her question affirmatively and expressed the hope that her hearers or readers would do the same. Doing so need not derogate from the special place that the Judeo-Christian scriptures allocate to human beings but would simply recognize that there is a whole spectrum of ways or degrees in which creatures might image forth their Creator. Accepting the existence of such a spectrum (a term which itself implies a continuum) could allow one to affirm a genuinely soul-like aspect to creatures other than humans and so avoid the need to posit the kind of "ontological leap" that Pope John Paul II referred to when noting the pronounced physical continuity that natural science affirms between human beings and other organisms. As Richard Swinburne said in his Gifford Lectures,

Talk about animal souls as well as human souls was normal in Greek philosophy and Christian medieval thought. The idea of a very sharp division between animals who had no souls, and men who had souls, arrived in the seventeenth century with Descartes and his strange view that animals were unconscious automata. Our experience is against that strange view. The difference between animals and men, as the medievals well recognized, was not that men had a mental life and so souls, and animals did not, but that men had a special kind of mental life (mental capacities that went beyond those of animals) and so a special kind of soul. The medievals called this soul the rational or intellectual soul, as opposed to the animal or sensitive soul.[58]

It was noted earlier that this last-named distinction was crucial for the medievals' attribution of immortality to the rational soul alone, but even this has been questioned in more recent times. In the eighteenth century, John Wesley remarked in one of his sermons that when the Book of Revelation speaks of God's ultimately making "all things new" (Rev. 21:5), "the following blessing shall take place (not only on the children of men; there is no such restriction in the text; but) on every creature according to its capacity: 'God shall wipe away all tears from their eyes. And there shall be no more death, neither sorrow, nor crying, neither shall there be any more pain: for the former things are passed away." Then, he adds, "the whole brute creation" will enjoy happiness "suited to their state, without alloy, without interruption, and without end."[59] More recently, others have made a similar argument on the basis of another scriptural text, the passage in Luke's Gospel where Jesus asks: "Are not five sparrows sold for two pennies? And not one of them is forgotten before God" (Lk. 12:6). Petroc and Eldred Willey suggest that since this divine "remembering" of creatures could be said to be the same as God's knowledge of them, and since being known by the eternal God could comprise immortality, then some kind of immortality might be available to creatures other than human beings alone.[60] The Greek Orthodox

theologian and bishop Kallistos Ware makes a similar point, referring to the same passage in Luke: "Was Greek Christianity justified
in denying immortality to animals? Christ says that not a single
sparrow is 'forgotten in God's sight'; God is concerned about the
death of each one of them (Luke 12:6; Matt. 10:29). Christ does
not say that sparrows have immortal life, but he does not deny
the possibility. If the New Testament leaves the question open,
should not we?"[61] One further text is often cited by authors who
are open to the possibility of some kind of everlasting life "with
God" on the part of other creatures, namely, Isaiah's vision of a
peaceable kingdom where the wolf and the lamb, the calf and the
young lion and all other creatures abide in harmony (Is. 11:6–
9). Commenting on this passage, Thomas Hosinski writes: "This
vision and promise allows us to hope that the highest aspect of
God's providential care — ultimate redemption and inclusion in
the everlasting life of God's 'kingdom' — will in fact be extended
to all God's creatures."[62]

None of these authors write apodictically, though they certainly
would object to dogmatic statements that some form of what the
Christian liturgy calls "everlasting life" is necessarily and certainly
reserved for human beings alone. A crucial phrase is surely one
found in the quotation from Wesley — "suited to their state," that
is, according to their capacity. It has long been common Christian
teaching that those who enjoy heavenly bliss "with the Lord" do
not all enjoy it in the same measure or to the same degree but
rather according to each one's capacity. A deceased infant would
not enjoy the *visio beatifica* in the same way as St. Francis of Assisi or St. Teresa of Avila. In one of the most beautiful passages
in Dante's *Paradiso,* the poet asks a saint in the lower region of
heaven if she is not envious of those who are still more exalted.
Piccarda replies: "Brother, the power of love quiets our will and
makes us wish only for that which we have and gives us no other
thirst....It is the essence of this blessed existence to keep itself
within the divine will, whereby our wills themselves are made one;
so that our being thus from threshold to threshold throughout this
realm is a joy to all the realm as to the King, who draws our wills

to what He wills; and in his will is our peace."[63] In the final analysis, theologians like Ware and Hosinski are asking us to reflect on the possibility that some degree of being "with the Lord" everlastingly may extend to creatures beyond the species *Homo sapiens*. However little urgency or "practical" value such reflections may seem to have, they at least open up the possibility that the *physical* continuity that has been so evident in scientific study of living beings can be understood philosophically and theologically as being reflected in a kind of *spiritual* continuity as well. At the very least, an openness to this avoids what one author has called "the plain absurdity, no less, of humans deciding for themselves which essential or substantial qualities qualify them for eternal life and which may or may not exclude animals. . . . Eternal life is God's own gift; it is not something which we can merit."[64]

None of this denies that the human person, body and soul, is a creature of God, but it does avoid the need to posit billions of direct divine interventions at or near the time of conception. Rather, one can reasonably argue that a God-given, soul-like aspect has characterized all forms of life from the beginning and that this aspect has been becoming more profound with evolutionary increases in complexity. It was surely an awareness of this aspect that allowed a saintly mystic like Francis of Assisi to address not only his fellow human beings but also the birds, the fish, and even a wolf as his true "brothers" and "sisters."

5

Cosmology and the
Doctrine of Eschatology

IN ONE OF the best-known passages in his *History of the English Church and People,* St. Bede the Venerable described a meeting that the Northumbrian King Edwin convened in the year 627. Edwin sought the advice of his counselors on the question of whether the faith being preached by the Christian missionary Paulinus should be accepted by the people. Among the speakers was one who compared the span of a human life to the flight of a sparrow through the royal banqueting hall on a wintry night. Inside the hall, warmth and light prevail, while a storm of rain and snow rages outdoors. The bird, he said, flies in through one door and out another. While inside the sparrow is safe from the storm, but after a short period of comfort "he vanishes from sight into the darkness whence he came. Similarly, man appears on earth for a little while, but we know nothing of what went before this life, and what follows. Therefore if this new teaching can reveal any more certain knowledge, it seems only right that we should follow it."[1] This argument prevailed with the king, who was shortly thereafter baptized together with his nobles and many of the commoners.

Bede's account addresses the mystery of individual human lives and the question of what might lie beyond the grave, an issue discussed in the preceding chapter of this book, but his narrative can also be read as pointing to the question of the life-span of our planet itself, and even of the universe as a whole. Can we rightly speak of the "death" of the earth, of the solar system, and of the entire cosmos? If so, then — in the language of the Northumbrian counselor — "what follows?" This is the kind of question traditionally addressed by Christian eschatology, and it will be the major focus of this chapter.

As already noted in chapter two, scientists now commonly hold that our universe began in a "big bang" some fifteen billion years ago, while our solar system was formed about ten billion years after that. The study of stars that are similar to the sun but considerably older gives a strong indication of what the future holds for the orb that provides almost all of our planet's light and heat. For example, the star Antares, more than 500 light-years away in the constellation Scorpio, was once the size of our sun but now, twice as old as the sun, has expanded to a vastly larger circumference as more and more of its hydrogen has fused into helium; indeed, the shell of plasma surrounding Antares is roughly the size of the earth's orbit. Its energy supply is being burnt up at an ever-faster rate and its cooling surface has become reddish, giving it and similar stars the name "red giants."[2] The same process is underway in the sun, leading the astrophysicist Arnold Benz to write: "How long the Sun will continue to shine can be predicted more surely than the weather in the coming month."[3] Specifically, cosmologists predict that the sun will be a red giant about six billion years from now and that, within a further billion years, its luminosity will increase by a factor of one thousand. Eventually it will reach a size one hundred times its present diameter, enough to fill the space now occupied by the planets Mercury and Venus, which will both be vaporized in the process. Earth itself will then have a surface temperature of over 1500° C., obliterating all traces of life. Subsequently the sun will become a white dwarf star, shrinking to the current size of the earth but with a density of about one ton per cubic centimeter and a temperature approaching absolute zero. One could appropriately speak of this situation as "the death of the solar system."

Similar language could be used of the universe as a whole, although scientists are much less certain about the details of its far distant future. For one thing, there are areas of the universe that have not yet been observed for the simple reason that there has not been sufficient time since the big bang for light from these regions to reach us, so nothing can be said with certainty about this as-yet-unseen domain. In fact, if the inflationary hypothesis is correct (according to which the very early universe underwent a brief period of extremely rapid expansion), then the universe is *immensely* larger than what is now observable. The science writer Timothy Ferris has tried to give some notion of this by a mind-boggling comparison: "If the entirety of an inflationary universe were the surface of the earth, the observable part would be smaller than a proton."[4]

With the whole field of modern cosmology still in its infancy, it is not surprising that there is as yet no firm consensus among scientists as to whether the universe will continue to expand or, under the force of gravity, contract back upon itself in what is sometimes called "the big crunch." Which scenario will occur depends largely on the amount of matter in the universe. At the present time, indications point to continuing, unending expansion. In fact, in early April of 2001 Adam Riess of the Space Telescope Science Institute and Peter Nugent of the Lawrence Berkeley National Laboratory announced that the study of light from the most distant supernova ever detected supports the theory that this expansion will occur at an accelerating rate.[5] If this is correct, even stars that are much more long-lived than the sun will all contract to white dwarfs in about 10^{14} years. Still much later than that, all the matter of the universe will have degenerated into a thin gas composed of subatomic photons and leptons "blowing around a framework of supermassive black holes,"[6] while the black holes will themselves gradually evaporate by so-called Hawking radiation. It is inconceivable that any organisms could live in that kind of environment. All of this raises the theological question of how the predicted demise of the universe might correlate with the traditional doctrine of Christian eschatology with its promise of "a new heaven and a new earth."

Not surprisingly, a number of thinkers see no correlation at all but take the somber predictions of scientific cosmology to be an ironclad refutation of that doctrine and of the hope that it inspires. Probably the best-known and most frequently quoted statement to this effect comes from the physicist Steven Weinberg, who claimed several decades ago that "the more the universe seems comprehensible, the more it also seems pointless."[7] A still more aggressive atheist, the Oxford professor of chemistry Peter Atkins, has written much more recently that "in due course, all matter will have decayed to radiation, all radiation will be stretched flat, and all there will be is dead flat space-time. All our achievements and aspirations will be as though they had never been."[8]

Common Theological Responses to the Prospect of Cosmic Death

Many theologians, while certainly not agreeing with the conclusions of Weinberg and Atkins, recognize the significant challenge that the projected death of the universe poses for religious believers. The following three — one German, one American, and one Scottish — are representative. Gerhard Sauter, director of the Ecumenical Institute at the University of Bonn, writes that "recent theories of cosmology agree that the world will come to an end either by slowly, yet certainly, growing cold — or just the other way: by progressive warming up and burning. The result seems to be the same: extermination.... [T]he general perspective of decay and disintegration has a paralyzing impact on the imagination, since it does not allow for any perspective beyond destruction, and we need such a perspective for our acting."[9] Similarly, Robert John Russell asks: "Are we really 'at home' in . . . a universe created and providentially cared for by God and guided to its ultimate purposes through God's redemptive love, if, as we now know, planetary extinction and, beyond this, the extinction of all life in the universe, is almost certainly what the far future promises?"[10] Lastly, John Macquarrie, writing some years before the most recent scientific data became available, claimed that "if it were shown that the universe is indeed headed for an all-enveloping death, then this might seem to constitute a state of affairs so wasteful and negative that it might be held to falsify Christian faith and abolish Christian hope."[11] Macquarrie was criticized by John Polkinghorne for making this "extreme" kind of statement,[12] but in his defense it should be noted that he immediately went on to say that he was possibly "not sufficiently recognizing the transcendence of God in relation to the creation or ... not sufficiently reckoning with the possibilities of transformation, for these, after all, must go far beyond what we can understand." Macquarrie's reference to "transformation," by which he means what scripture sometimes calls "a new heaven and a new earth" (Is. 65:17; 2 Pet. 3:13; Rev. 21:1), is most significant, for it is in terms of such transformation that many theologians have been trying to reconcile eschatological doctrine with the sobering scientific scenarios of either an endless cosmic expansion marked by ever-increasing entropy or a fiery contraction of massively obliterating force. I will examine the position of these theologians before looking at what I consider to be a more satisfactory alternative.

Those taking a transformationist approach include some of the most prominent theologians writing today. One of them is Jürgen Moltmann, who has dealt extensively with issues of eschatology ever since the publication of *The Theology of Hope* in 1967. His most recent book-length publication on the topic is *The Coming of God: Christian Eschatology,* published in German in 1995 and soon thereafter translated into other languages. Moltmann is by no means a fundamentalist in the way he approaches traditional Christian doctrine, but he is also unwilling to accept understandings of the human person that seem to leave no place for any kind of continued existence after life on earth. He accordingly criticizes Rosemary Radford Ruether for advocating the doctrine of "a natural death," at which "our existence ceases as individuated ego/organism and dissolves back into the cosmic matrix of matter/energy, from which new centers of individuation arise."[13] On the contrary, writes Moltmann, to agree with Ruether that we should have deep respect for "the good earth" does *not* also mean "giving ourselves up to burial with the consolation that we shall live on in worms and plants. It means waiting for the day when the earth will open, and the dead will rise, and the earth together with these dead will 'be raised' for its new creation."[14] As he writes earlier, human beings are so attached to the earth and the cosmos that there simply could be no redemption for us without some kind of redemption of the realm of nature as well, however impossible it may be to conceive just what "a new heaven and a new earth" would look like.[15]

John Polkinghorne, whose above-mentioned critique of Macquarrie itself gives a clue to what his position will be, has addressed this subject in a number of his publications, always in a way quite similar to Moltmann's position. In his Gifford Lectures, Polkinghorne spoke of "the new creation" as being "not a second attempt by God at what he first tried to do in the old creation. It is a different kind of divine action altogether.... [T]he new creation is the divine redemption of the old."[16] The transformationist theme is still more explicit in a recent paper on various issues in eschatology, where he says that "the matter of the new creation will be divinely transmuted matter."[17]

This terminology of "new creation" or "new world" is found regularly in theologians of a transformationist persuasion. Zachary Hayes, in reference to St. Paul's words about God's ability to "call into existence the things that do not exist" (Rom. 4:17), writes that "God does not annihilate his first creation in order to begin again from nothing. The 'new creation' of which eschatology speaks is here [in Paul] seen as the transforming completion of the fruit of God's first creative act."[18] Similarly, Ted Peters argues that "[if] the law of entropy has the last laugh and the cosmos drifts into a state of irrecoverable equilibrium ... then we would have proof that our faith has been in vain.... Our faith is allied with our hope, and our hope is based upon the promise ... that a new creation is coming by the grace and power of God."[19]

Whether by direct reference to particular scriptural passages or by more general allusions to a biblical promise of "a new heaven and a new earth" (Rev. 21:1; 2 Pet. 3:13), all of these theologians understandably base their conclusions on their interpretation of such passages. It is therefore crucial to consider whether the apocalyptic sections of the Bible definitely teach that the present universe will be divinely transformed "at the end of the ages." It goes without saying that the interpretation of apocalyptic texts is extremely difficult, not least because the very genre at times over-laps with prophecy, the distinction between the two being that prophecy generally looks *within* history for deliverance from an oppressive situation whereas apocalyptic sees the situation as so desperate as to call for what Raymond Brown has termed "direct divine intervention that will bring all to an end."[20] In Old Testament times, the Israelites' exile in Babylon in the sixth century B.C.E.. and the persecution of the Jews by the Seleucid monarch Antiochus IV Epiphanes four centuries later gave rise to apocalyptic writings, such as the Book of Daniel. The Roman occupation of Palestine and the destruction of the temple at Jerusalem in 70 C.E. were the occasion for still other apocalyptic writings, including the non-canonical books of IV Ezra and II Baruch. Whether in Jewish or Christian apocalypses, the secrets revealed to the human seer by one or more otherworldly beings typically "involve a cosmic transformation that will result in a transition from this world to a world or era to come and a divine judgment on all."[21]

The Book of Revelation, with which the New Testament con-cludes, is clearly this kind of work, the persecution now being not that of Jews by Babylonians or Seleucids but of Christians by pagan Rome, the city on seven hills (Rev. 17:9) symbolized by the harlot Babylon. The author's aim is to admonish his fel-low believers to stand firm in their faith, patiently awaiting the fulfillment of God's promise to wipe out all evildoers (21:8) and restore creation to a state of peace and harmony where there will be "no more death, neither shall there be mourning or crying or pain" (21:4). Edward Schillebeeckx observes in this regard that "the eschatological fullness" of this promised condition "can only be expressed in symbolic language, by speaking in parables and metaphors."[22] The apocalyptic images and metaphors must not be understood as scientifically precise predictions of some future state. Only then, writes New Testament scholar Gale Heide, will they be "freed to have their intended impact upon the audience," namely, to "give hope in the midst of despair, consolation in spite of persecution."[23] As Karl Rahner wrote in one of his most influential early essays, "the simplicity with which Scripture uses the most diverse imagery" shows that it "has no intention of describing the actual phenomena of the eschata themselves," as though the future already led a kind of supra-temporal existence.[24] Rahner's point is obvious enough with reference to an image like that of "a Lamb standing, as though it had been slain, with seven horns and with seven eyes" (Rev. 5:6), for it would be bizarre even to try to depict such a lamb literally. Most would surely agree with Rahner even with reference to images that are in themselves not quite so self-evidently symbolic but that could scarcely be made consistent with one another. His examples of mutually exclusive images include the following: people being gathered in the Valley of Jehoshaphat (Joel 3:2), the faithful being caught up in the clouds to meet the Lord in the air (1 Thess. 4:17), and the martyrs reigning with Christ for a thousand years on earth (Rev. 20:4).

No, the crucial issue lies elsewhere, in the very notion of "a new heaven and a new earth." Must this be understood as referring to a definite transformation of the present universe? In other words, is hope for some kind of (admittedly unimaginable) change in the physical cosmos the only way in which Christian faith can cope with contemporary science's prediction of an eventual and total cosmic demise? This seems to have been the assumption of John Macquarrie, with his fear that without some such transformation the prospect of "an all-enveloping death" would "constitute a state of affairs so wasteful and negative that it might be held to falsify Christian faith and abolish Christian hope." We have seen Lutheran theologian Ted Peters sharing the same basic fear: "if the law of entropy has the last laugh . . . then we would have proof that our faith has been in vain." The problem with such statements is that they may well belong to the same category as those assertions of seventeenth-century theologians who felt they could confidently judge the heliocentric system of Copernicus to be heretical because it contradicted what the Bible was assumed to be teaching about the sun's circular motion around a stationary earth. Tremendous harm was done to the Church when Galileo was convicted for holding and teaching this system, for we now see that he was much more adept at interpreting the Bible than were the theologians of his day. It could be equally misguided for theologians of the twenty-first century to reject the finality of scientific predictions of cosmic demise because they consider such a state to be incompatible with the teaching of scripture.[25] Does some other way lie open to theology?

An Alternative Theological Understanding of Cosmic Demise

One theologian who has recently suggested an alternative approach is Kathryn Tanner. She rightly notes how some of the religious thinkers referred to above have been able to avoid "a direct challenge from scientific end-time scenarios" by contesting the finality of the scientific description: whereas science predicts ultimate catastrophe for the physical universe, these theologians rest their case on God's power "to reverse those results, the power to bring what is otherwise absolutely unexpected into existence — say, a world that knows neither loss nor suffering."[26] Recalling that in the Middle Ages Aquinas was able to understand the doctrine of creation in such a way that it did not, as such, necessarily imply a temporal beginning of things, Tanner suggests that when there is a conflict between eschatology and scientific description, "one could, similarly, reinterpret the common contemporary outlook on eschatology so that it holds whatever [may be] the final state of the world, as scientifically described."[27] In the following paragraphs I will offer one such reinterpretation.

First, let me emphasize that even though I do not share the fears of Macquarrie and Peters that a cosmic state of irrecoverable equilibrium would constitute "proof that our faith has been in vain," and even though I consider such argumentation to be of the same general kind as that used by the theologians who condemned Galileo, it seems clear that no fully convincing counterargument is possible at this time. In the case of Galileo, it did not take many more decades before astronomical discoveries (such as the existence of stellar parallax) satisfactorily answered the major scientific objections to heliocentric theory. In the light of over-whelming evidence that the earth is among the planets orbiting the sun, theologians had no choice but to recognize that scriptural passages implying that the earth stands still while the sun moves around it could not be used to draw conclusions valid in the field of astronomy. The Bible came more and more to be seen for what it is: a religious work, not a scientific textbook. However, issues relating to the long-term future of the universe could not possibly be settled in the same way within the foreseeable future. Some years ago Rudolf Bultmann, referring to the fact that the parou-sia of Christ did not take place as soon as some New Testament writers expected, wrote: "History did not come to an end and, as every schoolboy knows, it will continue to run its course."[28] Bult-mann could be criticized for that use of the word *knows*, since one could never know for certain that history "will continue to run its course." Nevertheless, the vast majority of persons surely expect that it will and that the earth will continue orbiting the sun for sev-eral billion years until the latter body, vastly increasing in size and luminosity, renders our planet lifeless. Even if this occurs, as sci-entists predict, and even if after a very much longer period of time the universe disintegrates into an entropic state of low-grade radi-ation with a temperature approaching absolute zero, a theologian of our day could nevertheless claim, without fear of being proven wrong, that God could still transform this cosmic state of appar-ently irrecoverable equilibrium into that glorious "new heaven and new earth" of which certain passages in the Bible speak. For this reason, it should not be surprising if a number of theologians con-tinue to talk, with Polkinghorne, of "a new creation" composed of "divinely transmuted matter." I do, however, consider state-ments of this sort to be placing more weight on certain passages of scripture than the latter are able to bear.

Consider the phrase that frequently recurs in this context: "a new heaven and a new earth." One finds the expression already in the Book of Isaiah, specifically in that part composed after the Babylonian Exile and commonly referred to as Trito-Isaiah. There the Lord promises: "Lo, I am about to create new heavens and a new earth; the things of the past shall not be remembered or come to mind" (Is. 65:17). As one reads further, it becomes evident that this "new creation" is very much one that will be in continuity with the past, except that now "the sound of weeping shall no longer be heard there, or the sound of crying; there shall no longer be in it an infant who lives but a few days, or an old man who does not round out his full lifetime. He dies a mere youth who reaches but a hundred years, and he who fails of a hundred shall be thought accursed" (65:19–20). We surely ought not understand these verses as an exact prediction of some future state in which infant mortality will be utterly unknown; rather, they are words of hope and encouragement for a people who had just been through a devastating exile and were now yearning for a much better life as they returned to their homeland. But if this is how the passage from Isaiah should be interpreted — and it is in fact thus interpreted by scripture scholars — then surely the similar passage in the Book of Revelation would best be understood in a similar way, especially since much of its language reflects the Isaian passage and was no doubt influenced by it (for example, "neither shall there be mourning nor crying nor pain any more" [Rev. 21:4]). To take the verse about "a new heaven and a new earth" out of the context of providing hope and encouragement to Christians suffering oppression from the Romans — and of still being able to provide hope to people today by assuring them that even the worst of human situations do not remove them from the realm of God's love — and to see it instead as predicting an eventual transformation of the physical universe seems quite unwarranted. The hermeneutic key for understanding apocalyptic texts like the Book of Revelation was succinctly expressed by Raymond Brown, one of the most highly respected scripture scholars of the twentieth century, in the following words: "Because its visions are filled with theological symbols, not with photographic reproductions, [the Book of Revelation] does not give an exact knowledge of that other world, a world that cannot be translated into human concepts. Rather, it attests forcefully that at every moment of human history, even the most desperate moment that causes people to lose hope, God is present."[29]

Brown's guideline complements another that was enunciated by John Polkinghorne in his Gifford Lectures when he said: "I do not think that the eventual futility of the universe, over a time-scale of tens of billions of years, is very different in the theological problems it poses, from the eventual futility of ourselves, over a timescale of tens of years. Cosmic death and human death pose equivalent questions of what is God's intention for his creation. What is at issue is the faithfulness of God."[30] This insight opens up the possibility of bringing together reflections on human death from the previous chapter of this book with the present discussion of cosmic demise. Just as I there argued that the entry of a holy person into eternal life "body and soul" need not involve the transposition of that person's corporeal remains into some other realm, so too it does not seem to me at all necessary to assert that the scriptural promise of "a new creation" is incompatible with a universe moving endlessly into a state of greater and greater entropy (sometimes called by the ambiguous term "heat death" because there would eventually be no heat at all). As noted earlier, there is no possible way to say for certain that such a state of irrecoverable equilibrium will in fact occur, even though many scientists now consider this likely. My main point is simply to caution against theological assertions that the physical universe could not possibly end up in such a final state on the grounds that this would be contrary to scripture. Whereas Moltmann has claimed that because there is "no humanity detached from nature — from life, the earth and the cosmos — there . . . can be no eternal life for human beings without the change in the cosmic conditions of life,"[31] it seems to me that more theological tentativeness is in order. While one could readily assert that Christian faith clearly includes a call for human beings to be "with God" beyond the grave, and while I have earlier suggested that this *may* extend, *mutatis mutandis,* to other beings possessing some degree of consciousness, there seems to be far less warrant to include inanimate entities in this call. One of the most constant themes in the spiritual teaching of the world's religious traditions is that human beings ought not to cling to possessions of one sort or another and that things will in fact normally be much more appreciated and enjoyed if one does not cling to them or yearn for them to have a permanence that is not appropriate. William Blake expressed this in a memorable short poem entitled "Eternity":

> He who binds to himself a joy
> Does the winged life destroy;
> But he who kisses the joy as it flies
> Lives in eternity's sun rise.

May it not be that these lines also say something about God's relationship to inanimate nature? May not the latter give joy to its Creator even if, as many scientists believe, it is moving toward an irreversible demise? The main point of this chapter is that it would, at the very least, be wise to leave this question open. One further point must nevertheless be addressed: Some religious thinkers fear that accepting the possibility that there will be no literal, divinely inaugurated "new creation" will inevitably devalue the world around us and contribute to the environmental problems that already loom so large in our world. The final section of this chapter will address this important issue.

Human Concern for the World around Us

Among those who have addressed questions relating to the long-term prospects for the universe, Willem Drees has underscored how unrealistic it can be to speculate too much on matters billions or trillions of years in the future. He accordingly wishes to direct attention to issues of how we ought to relate to the world today.[32] Other theologians and scientists have likewise been trying to raise awareness of this matter. Gerhard Sauter draws attention to a sentence mistakenly attributed to Luther: "If I knew that tomorrow the world would end, I would still plant an apple tree today."[33] Whoever may have first penned this sentence, it does express something very important about the eschatological theme of hope against hope. Hope for "a new creation" ought not be limited to some expectation that God alone will bring this about. In fact, it is *this* expectation that could well give rise to human complacency and passivity. On the contrary, as Wilfrid Harrington observes in his commentary on the Book of Revelation, "God has freely, from the start, involved mankind in his creation. In his plan a new world for humankind can only come about with human involvement."[34] A key question is, What kind of involvement? Some environmentalists are especially wary of any activity in this area by persons in the Judeo-Christian tradition, since they feel that this tradition has been responsible for many of the problems in the first place.

Their suspicion derives in large measure from a short, simplistic, but very influential article by Lynn White Jr., first published in 1967 and frequently reprinted in anthologies and other works.[35] Although White's approach is somewhat more nuanced than is often thought by persons who have not actually read his article, he does make a sharp distinction between the Judeo-Christian tradition and the paganism that it largely replaced in much of the Western world. He writes, for example, that Christianity inherited from Judaism a story of creation in which all other creatures on earth — the plants, animals, birds, and fish — were made by God "explicitly for man's benefit and rule: no item in the physical creation had any purpose save man's purposes."[36] Whereas in ancient paganism every tree, spring, stream, and hill had its guardian spirit that had to be placated before one cut a tree, mined a mountain, or dammed a brook, Christianity, "by destroying pagan animism...made it possible to exploit nature in a mood of indifference to the feelings of natural objects.... Man's effective monopoly on spirit in this world was confirmed, and the old inhibitions to the exploitation of nature crumbled."[37]

White speaks of himself in the article as a churchman and is definitely not critical of all aspects of the Christian tradition. For one thing, he suggests that the more contemplative tenor of the Eastern Christian Church meant that a spirit of conquering nature emerged more easily in the Western Church. Even in the West he finds a significant resource for a sound ecology in the example of

St. Francis of Assisi, who, he says, tried to substitute the idea of the equality of all creatures for the idea of humanity's limitless rule over the rest of creation. He concludes his piece by proposing St. Francis as a patron saint for ecologists, something that Pope John Paul II subsequently affirmed. The rightness of this choice of patron is related to a point I made at the conclusion of the previous chapter — Francis's readiness to see not only his fellow human beings but also other forms of life as his brothers and sisters. In this he was, without of course being aware of it, going beyond what is nowadays called "a stewardship model" (by which humans are seen as having a duty to care for the rest of the earth) to what Elizabeth Johnson and others term "a kinship model," which "sees human beings and the earth with all its creatures [as being] intrinsically related as companions in a community of life."[38] One may not learn from someone like Francis a lot of specific details about how to relate to the rest of nature today but one can receive from him something still more important, what the Lutheran theologian Paul Santmire calls a foundational theological vision "that envisions a close ontological bond between God and humans, on the one hand, and nature, on the other; that presupposes an understanding of God that readily highlights those qualities of the divine life that show God as immanent in and as befriending all creatures and that, accordingly, encourages humans to do the same."[39]

Encouragement of this sort is probably more necessary than the acquisition of specialized knowledge, though this too is very necessary. As Patricia Mische, co-founder of Global Education Associates, has written: "Many [people] feel powerless in the face of the enormity and complexity of the issues today. We stand in this time and space, at a place in history where we are personally and collectively being asked to respond to life and death questions about the future of humanity; ...and we may look at ourselves and ask, 'Who are we?' Are we capable of becoming, and living responsibly in, a *world* community?"[40] The only proper response to her questions is to see them not as obstacles to be feared but as opportunities to be embraced, knowing that if we as individuals live in an ecologically responsible way, sensing our kinship with the rest of the created order, we will in fact be living more vibrant and wholesome lives regardless of how many other people do or do not follow suit. The Belgian moral theologian Roger Burggraeve expresses in a balanced way the relationship between the divine and human aspects of working for a new creation when he writes that the promise of "a new world" is "not just a promise for a 'remote' or ultimate future which we shall receive gratis — in superabundant grace — from God, but at the same time means a radical questioning of our present relationship with the world. In this respect, the promise of the new world also contains an urgent ethical task, the need . . . to be converted and — in the power of the promise — even now to work on the new world held in prospect for us."[41] Whatever be the final end of our planet, of the solar system, and of the cosmos as a whole, what faces us *now* is a planet much more fragile than earlier generations believed. Some of the environmental damage that has already been done may well be irreversible, resulting from what Pope John Paul II has called "the behavior of people who show a callous disregard for the hidden, yet perceivable requirements of the order and harmony which govern nature itself."[42] Other damage, however, can still be corrected, provided that enough people work together under strong leadership and in a scientifically informed way on the local, national, and international levels. To revert to the imagery of St. Bede at the beginning of this chapter, we may not be able to foresee exactly the long-range cosmic future that lies in the darkness outside the royal banqueting hall, but there is certainly enough light within the hall for people of good will to make a difference during the time allotted them on earth.

6

The Causal Continuum of Space-Time Events and Divine Action

THE PRECEDING CHAPTERS of this book have referred to various issues concerning traditional understandings of God's relationship with the world, whether as its creator, providential guide, or salvific goal. This relationship has traditionally been construed as an *active* one. Within the Judeo-Christian scriptures, there are numerous accounts of what are often called "the mighty acts of God": the accounts of creation in the opening chapters of the Book of Genesis, the narrative of the exodus of the Israelites from Egypt (when God sent plagues upon the Egyptians, led the Israelites to safety by cleaving a path through the Red Sea, and then cared for them in their desert wanderings by making water flow forth from rock and raining manna upon the people for their food), and — for Christians the divine act *par excellence* — the sending of the Son, Jesus Christ, as savior of the world. Many of the Psalms go into great detail about God's deeds, whether acts on behalf of the nation as a whole or ones for individuals in distress (such as Ps. 107), leading the Psalmist to exclaim at one point: "How manifold are your works, O Lord! In wisdom you have wrought them all" (Ps. 104:24). Of course, believers do not hold that God's deeds were limited to biblical times. Countless prayers seeking God's aid are offered daily by people all over the world, while one of the basic assumptions of the widespread practice of spiritual direction is that persons can be helped to be-

112

come more and more aware of ways in which God is at work in their lives. It would not be an exaggeration to claim that in all of the major theistic traditions, God is firmly believed to be *a God who acts.*

For many centuries this belief was generally unproblematic. Even today it is at the very center of the thought of some of the world's leading theologians. In a recent interview Wolfhart Pannenberg, reflecting on some of the major influences on his own thought, singled out the work of the Old Testament scholar Gerhard von Rad for this very reason. Von Rad, he said, "was able to speak of the stories of the Old Testament as if they were about real life — much more real than the secular life that we experience otherwise.... His thesis, that God is acting with Israel and with all humanity in history and that history is constituted by the acts of God, has influenced me more than any other thing that I learned as a student."[1] On the other hand, another prominent theologian, Langdon Gilkey, pointed out some years ago that other scripture scholars of our time were not nearly so clear about what God did in and for ancient Israel. Gilkey noted that if one had asked a premodern theologian like John Calvin what he believed God did at the Exodus, the answer would have been clear: "Look at the Book of Exodus and see what it says that God did." When one reads Calvin's commentary on that part of the Bible, he recounts God's deeds just as they appear in the scriptural text. How different, remarks Gilkey, is what many scripture scholars of the past fifty years say (or do not say) in reply to the question: "What did God actually do in the Exodus-Sinai event?" He finds the answer of scholars like G. E. Wright and Bernhard Anderson "extremely elusive to discover," for they assert "that outwardly the event was indistinguishable from other events, revelation to the Hebrews always being dependent on faith," and they also claim "that probably there was a perfectly natural explanation of the objective side of the event," such as a strong east wind driving back shallow waters in a marshy area and so allowing the Israelites to walk across to freedom, whereas the chariot wheels of their Egyptian pursuers became clogged in the mud.[2]

Gilkey was not castigating these authors for their reticence to say what God actually did, for modern science has so imbued the Western mind with a keen sense of an unbroken and unbreakable causal nexus in space and time that "modern theologians and scholars...can scarcely do anything else."[3] Nevertheless, this reluctance or inability to say anything very definite about God's activity does raise major issues for members of theistic religious traditions. In the words of one philosopher of religion, "Of what use is a God who cannot really change the course of history or nature, who does not causally explain the existence of life or the universe, or who cannot be causally effective in the process of redemption?"[4] The issue is not merely one of asking whether God could "unmake the laws of nature" by intervening on special occasions to bring about certain divinely willed results. One must also bear in mind that any change in the natural world necessarily involves an input of physical energy and this raises the question of how a spiritual, unembodied reality could bring about such an effect in our space-time continuum. As Philip Clayton has written, "if a spiritual agent gives rise to a physical effect, it has brought about physical change without a physical cause or the expenditure of physical energy, and this fractures the natural order in a way that would make science impossible."[5] Many people can no doubt shrug off this kind of issue simply by contending that anything is possible for an all-powerful God, but theologians and philosophers who have pondered the matter are keenly aware of the profundity of the questions involved. One scholar has recently gone so far as to say that "of all the challenges science has raised for theology, perhaps the most fundamental is that it has brought into question the doctrine of divine action."[6] Four decades earlier, one of the most influential writers on the topic, William Pollard, avowed that "I found extraordinary difficulty, when I thought about events in scientific terms, in imagining any kind of loophole through which God could influence them."[7] The purpose of this chapter is to describe some of the major ways in which theologians have dealt with this challenge and to suggest what seems to me the most satisfactory response.

Some Ways of Approaching the Issue of Divine Action

One obvious way out of the difficulty is simply to abandon talk of God's directly acting in the world. One need not be an atheist to adopt this approach, for it also characterized the Christian existentialism of Rudolf Bultmann, whose 1941 essay "New Testament and Mythology" became very influential and has often been anthologized.[8] The key to his solution to the problem was to draw a sharp distinction between the kind of knowledge available to us through scientific endeavor and the kind made available through Christian faith. For Bultmann the Judeo-Christian scriptures were not to be understood as giving anything like an objective world picture but rather as showing how we humans are to understand ourselves in our world. By this move, "Bultmann reinterpreted all talk of God's action in particular events in terms of the way in which they open up new possibilities for understanding human existence when perceived with the eyes of faith. God's action is confined to the inner level of personal address and existential challenge rather than to the external level of factual explanation."[9] This limitation on God's action to "the inner level of personal address" may indeed be considered preferable to an atheistic denial of all such action and even to the deistic position of claiming that God set everything in motion "at the beginning of time" but has not been active in the subsequent evolution of the universe or in the events of history, but Bultmann's approach so severely curtails the scope of divine action that many theologians have sought alternative understandings. The latter have at times arisen precisely out of an awareness of scientific findings that were unavailable to Bultmann, whose strictly deterministic view of the natural world is no longer considered viable by many scientists. Three prominent alternatives will be examined in turn: top-down or downward causality (also known as "whole-part influence"), bottom-up causality (relying on quantum theory, sometimes in conjunction with chaos theory), and primary-secondary causality.

The term "downward causation" was first used several decades ago by Donald Campbell and since that time has consistently been advocated by the physical biochemist and theologian Arthur Peacocke to elucidate the question of how God acts in the world.[10] Whereas the notion of causality in science has usually been described in terms of the "bottom-up" effect of the properties and behavior of a system's constituent units on the properties and behavior of the system as a whole, it is nowadays more and more clearly seen that the decisive factors in a system's behavior may move in the other direction as well. Noting that in certain reaction systems "thousands of molecules in a particular region at a particular time suddenly change to another form," Peacocke wrote in the early 1990s that these changes at the micro-level of molecular organization "are what they are *because* of their incorporation into the system as a whole, which is exerting specific constraints on its units, making them behave otherwise than they would in isolation."[11] More recently, Peacocke has moved away from the language of causation in describing this kind of phenomenon because the latter does not allow for description in terms of temporal, linear chains of causality of the type "A causes B, which in turn causes C," and so on. For this reason, he now prefers the term "whole-part influence" to describe the effects on the constituent parts of their being incorporated into systems of this kind, as when certain autocatalytic reaction systems spontaneously display rhythmic and spatial patterns whose forms can even depend on the very size of the vessel that contains them.[12] But even with his move away from the language of causality, Peacocke nevertheless still maintains that this kind of "downward" influence can illuminate an understanding of how God acts upon the natural world. A central point undergirding his argument is that we ought to place much more emphasis on divine immanence than was often the case in traditional theology, where the divine transcendence was understood in such a way as to leave a vast abyss between God and the created order. If, argues Peacocke, we consistently stress that all created things are truly *in* God — a position which Christian theology can readily support on the basis of such scriptural texts as Paul's quoting to the Athenians the poetic verse that "in him [God] we live and move and have our being" (Acts 17:28) — then it would not be unreasonable to look upon God as the "System-of-systems," the overarching context of all reality. As such, and precisely because the world is "in God," God could have a genuine influence on inner-worldly patterns and behaviors just as, analogously, a containing vessel can affect the patterns and behaviors of the units within it. Beyond the emphasis on God's immanence, Peacocke's position also assumes that "the omniscient God uniquely knows... everything that it is possible to know about the state(s) of all that is, including the interconnectedness and interdependence of the world's entities, structures, and processes."[13] On the basis of this assumption, he goes on to argue that God's particular intentions for certain events to occur can truly be effective, even events intended by God in response to human actions or prayers. To be sure, Peacocke does not claim that this explains exactly how God can bring about events in the natural world, for since "God's own Being is distinct from anything we can possibly know in the world, then God's nature is ineffable and will always be inaccessible to us, so that we have only the resources of analogy to depict *how* God might influence events."[14] Still, the Oxford scientist-theologian believes that his approach, based on an analogy drawn from observable scientific phenomena, can help elucidate traditional religious convictions about God's action in the world without requiring divine interventions that would violate that causal nexus whose existence is a basic assumption of modern science.

Another prominent scholar in the science-theology dialogue, Philip Clayton, also makes use of a general notion of downward causation, though with emphases somewhat different from those of Peacocke. The thought of both these authors is still evolving, but the overall lines of Clayton's position may be gleaned from his book *God and Contemporary Science,* especially the final two chapters. Here he commends Peacocke for speaking of God's action holistically and for avoiding a position that would have divine action be intermittent or sporadic, but he feels that the British scholar's top-down theory of divine agency can usefully be supplemented by thinking more carefully about a basic analogy between human and divine action.[15] Specifically, he suggests that reflection on the phenomenon of human mental causation — the question of how human intentions bring about events in the world around us — permits us to argue that God's action could be construed in an analogous way. In developing his argument both in his book and in a more recent essay, Clayton eschews any talk of the mind as being a separate substance altogether distinct from the body, but he also rejects a "strong reductionist" position that human thought is in principle fully explainable by neuronal firings within the brain. His own mediating position regards personhood as representing an explanatory level that is distinct from explanations at the physical level of our body or brain even though it presupposes the physical. In other words, mental phenomena are dependent on but not reducible to physical characteristics, the latter characteristics being necessary but not sufficient conditions for the former. Clayton emphasizes that his position does not require one to accept the truth of theism — mental causation can still be explained in this-worldly terms, "although at least part of the explanation will have to employ irreducibly psychological concepts."[16] This means, in turn, that the conscious or mental dimension of the human person not only exists but also exerts genuinely causal efficacy, and for his argument this is enough to ground the analogy with divine action: God can be understood to act on any part of the world in a way similar to (though not strictly identical with) our action on our bodies.

Although there are still other thinkers who advocate one or another kind of top-down causality, the two whose positions are described above suffice to show the general lines of this position. Without denying the value of this approach, at least as a subsidiary part of a larger whole, other authors place more emphasis on the opposite end of the causal spectrum by speculating that God could affect even the smallest constituent parts of the universe in such a way as to eventually effect changes on the macro-level. One of the most attractive options for these authors is found in quantum theory, which according to many scientists shows that the subatomic world is essentially indeterministic: micro-particles do have their distinguishing characteristics, but it is not possible to predict just when they will do whatever they do.[17] This degree of uncertainty seems to provide an intrinsic opening for God to act within the limits of quantum uncertainty without violating any physical laws. Two scholars — the cosmologist George Ellis and the theologian Nancey Murphy — have written extensively on this, at times in collaboration with one another.[18] One of Ellis's main concerns focuses on a particular kind of purported divine action, namely, how God might communicate images of God's own reality or of the underlying purpose of the universe to human beings through some kind of revelation. Since quantum theory does not (and apparently cannot) predict the result of any particular physical event, Ellis suggests that God could provide specific images to individuals or stimulate specific memories that already exist in someone's memory "by controlling the specific energy exchanges between particular excited states in the brain, without violating quantum mechanics in any way."[19]

Murphy makes a similar suggestion by proposing that God could affect human consciousness "by stimulation of neurons [in the brain]. . . . Such stimulation would cause thoughts to be recalled to mind; presumably it could cause the occurrence of new thoughts by coordinated stimulation of several ideas, concepts, or images stored in memory."[20] She suggests that the concatenation of such phenomena is what constitutes revelation. Despite their similarity on this point, Ellis and Murphy do diverge on how extensive this kind of divine influence may be. Ellis proposes that God has voluntarily limited divine activity in this world to three kinds of action: the initial creation of the universe and the setting of its initial conditions; the unique event of the manifestation of God's nature through the life of Christ; and direct actions by way of mental interventions, as described above. Accordingly, he rules out other kinds of action on God's part, such as preventing some natural disaster in answer to prayer.[21] Murphy, on the other hand, does not accept such limits. Since the behavior of macro-level objects is largely (though not exclusively) determined by the behavior of their smallest constituents, God's capacity to act on the former must include the ability to act on the latter. While one could, with Ellis, argue that the latter kind of action is restricted to certain kinds of events, Murphy disagrees. The majority view within the Christian tradition has been that God acts in all things at all times, and she makes this view part of her own approach. God is accordingly a participant not only "in *every* (macro-level) event" but also in countless quantum-level events, for God's participation in the former "is *by means of* his governance of the quantum events that *constitute* each macro-level event."[22] Rather than hold, with some scientists, that the "when" of quantum events is completely random, Murphy contends that "the better option is divine determination."[23] Considering that a single cubic centimeter of water is composed of 3.34×10^{22} molecules (and of even more atoms and subatomic particles) and that the number of neurons in a human brain is far larger than that, it is easy to see why her position has been called "very robust,"[24] and "a bold systematic attempt to develop a coherent theology of divine action."[25]

All of the positions described thus far — the top-down proposals of Peacocke and Clayton and the bottom-up ones of Ellis and Murphy — very consciously and with considerable expertise rely on various findings of modern science, such as the effect of systems as a whole on their constituent parts (as in certain chemical or biological events) or the influence of quantum-level events on the macro-world. The third general position that I will describe — that of primary-secondary causality — is less bound to specific scientific observations and more closely related to an older philosophical tradition, but its contemporary adherents nevertheless find it most valuable for considering divine action in a modern context. Like the other two positions, it grants a considerable degree of autonomy to the natural order, though without necessarily ruling out the possibility of occasional divine interventions of a miraculous sort. As classically expounded by Thomas Aquinas, this position holds that God, as the ultimate cause of the natural order, confers upon things their form, movement, and efficacy and, *in this sense,* is the primary cause of every event. This efficacy or power is, on the other hand, truly given to things, and because it belongs to them, they, as secondary causes, can rightly be said to perform their operations.

When treating this matter in his *Summa Contra Gentiles,* Aquinas acknowledged that some people find it difficult to understand how natural effects can be attributed to both God and a natural agent, since it seems contradictory at first hearing to say that one and the same action proceeds from two agents. He replies that this objection is easily resolved once it is understood that in every agent two points are to be considered: the thing itself that acts and the power by which it acts. "The power of a lower agent depends on the power of a superior agent, according as the superior agent gives this power to the lower agent whereby it may act." Therefore, "it is not inappropriate for the same effect to be produced by a lower agent and by God: by both immediately, though in different ways *(ab utroque immediate, licet alio et alio modo)."*[26] This means that it is not a matter of an action being done partly by God and partly by a natural agent; rather, the action is done wholly by both, though in different respects.[27] Moreover, the fact that God thereby works in and through secondary causes is not to be understood as a deficiency on God's part but rather as a sign of the divine goodness. As Etienne Gilson once phrased it, "The universe, as represented by St. Thomas, is not a mass of inert bodies passively moved by a force which passes through them but a collection of active beings each enjoying the efficacy delegated to it by God along with actual being."[28] Even though Aquinas formulated this position centuries before the rise of current issues about divine action in the world, those who have today adopted his position consider it to be one of great merit. Elizabeth Johnson has gone so far as to claim that Aquinas's understanding of the relationship between God and the world "accommodates evolutionary science with almost surprising ease. For the basic principle remains the same: God's providential guidance is accomplished in and through the free working of secondary causes."[29] The next section of this chapter will evaluate this as well as the other two general positions described above.

An Evaluation of the Three Alternative Approaches

I want to emphasize at the very beginning of this section that I fully agree with Peacocke's assertion, noted above, that since God's nature is ineffable, we have only the resources of analogy when considering how God might influence events. This theme of the incomprehensibility of God's nature (which is *not* the same as saying that we can have no valid knowledge of God at all) has a long pedigree in Christian theology and must be kept in mind as we examine the various analogies that were described in the preceding section of this chapter. To say that a comparison or analogy limps is not to render it valueless. However, it is also incumbent on theologians to seek the best analogies possible and to state why some are preferable to others, as I shall do in what follows.

Peacocke and Clayton both emphasize the interrelationship between their proposals and a doctrine of panentheism, the position that the created order, "the world," is within the all-encompassing God and yet distinct from God (this last point being the key difference between pan*en*theism and pantheism). This seems especially crucial for Peacocke's way of arguing for a whole-part influence, analogous to the way the behavior of the constituent parts of certain systems are affected by the characteristics of the system itself. Even though he no longer wants to use the language of cause and effect for this kind of phenomenon in the physical order, it does seem valid to speak of the influence of the whole on the individual parts, and in this respect it is reasonable for him to draw a comparison between this and the way an all-embracing God may influence beings or events in the created order. There are, however, weaknesses with this analogy as well. For one thing, the physical phenomena to which he refers (such as the so-called Bénard phenomenon, according to which individual molecules in a hexagonal cell will at a certain point start moving with a common velocity in a coordinated way) are characterized by having all of the constituent parts affected in the same way by the system as a whole, whereas a viable doctrine of divine action would certainly want to allow for diverse effects on the individuals concerned. Another problematic question has been raised by Clayton in his generally sympathetic analysis of Peacocke's proposal, for he asks how significant God's guidance could be if it comes to individuals in a highly mediated fashion, that is, in a top-down hierarchy "proceeding from the universe-as-a-whole, down through superstrings and galaxies to our individual planet, and then through the history of biological evolution and countless billions of genetic mutations to one person existing today?"[30] In other words, the proposal seems to imply a very attenuated kind of influence, not what one generally expects from a doctrine of divine action.

Clayton's own suggestion, likewise based on panentheistic assumptions, draws on our experience of being able intentionally to affect our own behavior. There is an obvious attractiveness of this for persons within religious traditions such as Judaism and Christianity, in which the personal aspects of divine reality are emphasized. The Bible regularly speaks of God as desiring certain ends and seeing that they do in fact occur, even as we experience the ability to bring about some of the results we desire. On this analogy, some theologians even speak of the created order as being in some way God's body.[31] However, using the mind-body analogy to elucidate the reality of divine action has a decided liability: Clayton, along with the large majority of contemporary thinkers, rejects the dualism of understanding the mind as a separate substance, whereas he must retain some kind of God-world dualism if his panentheism is not to lapse into outright pantheism. Clayton himself is well aware of the problem, for he notes in the final pages of his book that even though he argues that God can act on any part of our world "in a way similar to our action on our bodies," nevertheless Christian faith holds that "God also transcends the world" in a way that the mind does not transcend the body. Even as he has sought to describe a faith stance "that is as informed and as critical as it is possible to be," still "theological assertions never fully divest themselves of a component of faith and trust.... The transcendence of God can no more be 'read off' the world than ... the eschaton [can be] demonstrated on the basis of our knowledge of physical cosmology."[32]

In my opinion, the limitations of the analogies advocated by Peacocke and Clayton are minimal compared to those advanced by the bottom-up proposals of Ellis and Murphy. Both of the latter suggest that God could cause certain thoughts to arise in our minds by the stimulation of particular neurons in the brain. While Ellis's proposal excludes other forms of divine action (apart from the initial creation of the universe and what Christian faith considers the unique event of the manifestation of God's nature in Jesus Christ), Murphy goes much further, proposing "divine determination" of *every* macro-level event by way of God's "governance" of the micro-level quantum events that constitute the former. This could be considered a "safe" proposal in the sense that there seems to be no way of proving that divine action does not occur at this level. Ellis recognizes this when he writes that even though he expects his proposal to be "unpalatable" to many physicists and philosophers, nevertheless "if asked to disprove it, they will be unable to do so, for it does not in any way conflict with the foundations of modern physics."[33] For a proposal to be truly successful, however, it surely has to be seen as plausible, not merely "possible" and unable to be disproven. Any analogy for divine action should not only be compatible with our understanding of the natural world but also in accord with a traditional understanding of God, and this is where I find the analogy weak. Commenting on the quantum-based argument, Clayton has written that Robert J. Russell, who has influenced the thought of Murphy and others, "has been a leading advocate of the view that God could intervene supernaturally within the scope of quantum indeterminacy. Given billions and billions of such minute interventions . . . God *might* be able to effect significant changes on the macroscopic level."[34] My only reservation with this statement is that the phrase "billions and billions" is actually a gross understatement, given that at least this many quantum events take place every few seconds within a single person's brain or within a cubic centimeter of any material object. The analogy seems to require that God be envisioned as some kind of micro-managing ultra-supercomputer, literally "governing" or "determining" an unfathomable number of events on the smallest conceivable scale throughout the entire universe. I submit that this is not a plausible way of understanding what the best of the Christian tradition has meant by God's omnipotence and omniscience. We cannot, of course, speak of divine knowledge and power except on the basis of some analogy with the human instantiation of these traits, always recognizing that the divine instantiation transcends the human. Nevertheless, it is perhaps worth noting that we would not consider a human being admirably knowledgeable if he or she knew all sorts of minutiae about the world in which we live, such as how many words (or atomic particles) there are in a certain book. Similarly, we would not admire the "power" of a civil or religious leader who was in complete control of the most minute workings of every aspect of his or her organization, as distinct from someone who delegated tasks to others at a more appropriate level. This is a major reason why I find the notion of a micro-managing deity unsatisfactory.

Another reason for my uneasiness with the proposals of writers like Ellis and Murphy concerns the ability of individual quantum-level inputs to bring about significant changes at the macro-level in the first place. In some way activity at the quantum-level would have to be amplified, and chaos theory is sometimes invoked as one way of helping explain how minute changes in initial conditions can lead to massive effects in a relatively short period of time.[35] The example often used is the flapping of a butterfly's wings:[36] some writers place the small creature in Beijing and suggest that its flapping can produce a storm in New York some days later, while others locate the insect in Brazil and the resulting downpour in Texas. Similarly, the argument runs, events introduced by divine intention at the quantum level may be ramified by chaos effects to produce phenomena readily observable by our unaided senses. This line of reasoning, however, is not only counter-intuitive but simply wrong. The phrase "butterfly effect" was coined in the 1960s by the meteorologist Edward Lorenz, but his intent was "to describe the behaviour inside one of a series of parallel horizontal convection rolls"; as such, the butterfly effect "actually counts *against* butterfly-sized causes producing tornado-like effects. For the model assumes that the large-scale pattern of rolls, laid side by side like so many felled logs, remains entirely stable; the chaotic behaviour is local...."[37] In the same way, random quantum events "are washed out in the macroscopic realm and cannot serve as the foundation for a sufficiently rich model of divine agency."[38] It would therefore seem best to leave the small butterfly and its miniscule local effects in Beijing (or Brazil) and also to be dubious about using chaos theory to help explain the necessary amplification of quantum-level effects when advancing an argument for divine action. In sum, as one philosopher of science has written, "Simply saying that God influences quantum mechanics is not enough — we must further consider how this action could be consistent with our current understanding of the theory.... The onus is upon theologians to look at quantum mechanics in all its technical detail in order to substantiate their claims.... The implications of the various alternatives quantum theory offers are not as simple as many theologians have assumed."[39]

The final proposal to be evaluated is that of primary-secondary causality. As already noted, Aquinas recognized that it may appear contradictory to speak of two different agents as causes of one and the same effect. Even though he answered this objection to his own satisfaction, not everyone agrees. John Polkinghorne has criticized this theory of "double agency," at least as it was formulated in several books by Austin Farrer, as "theological doublespeak,"[40] while David Ray Griffin objects that this approach assumes the sufficiency of each cause and that the idea of two sufficient causes for one event is unacceptable.[41] These objections do not appear convincing. It does not seem "doublespeak" to acknowledge that divine causality and that of a natural agent exert their causality in different respects (Aquinas's *alio et alio modo*), and if this is so, then there seems to be no need to regard them in terms of necessary and/or sufficient causality. To be sure, neither Aquinas nor any of his modern followers contend that this understanding of causality does away with the need to affirm the mysteriousness of God's reality and activity, but Elizabeth Johnson is surely correct in emphasizing that this approach has the distinct advantage of avoiding any notion that God is "simply a bigger and better secondary cause. [Rather,] the distinction between primary and secondary causality enables thought to hold firm to the mystery of the Godness of God and the integrity of creatures, seeing both acting in a unique *concursus*."[42] Like the proposals of Ellis and Murphy, this one, too, is "safe" inasmuch as one could not rightly be challenged to detect the divine primary cause by empirical methods, for according to this theory there are no "pure secondary causes" that would make possible a "control experiment" allowing us to see what difference the added ingredient of divine primary causality would make.[43] This is not a drawback to the approach, however, since relatively few thinkers today would even want to argue that particular divine actions are discernible *as such* by the empirical methods of natural science.

A problem does arise, however, if too much is claimed for the primary-secondary distinction. Johnson writes at one point in her article that "God's providential guidance is accomplished in and through the free working of secondary causes."[44] In one sense a religious believer could not but agree with this statement, but it should be noted that this is a statement of one's belief that, in the words of the medieval English mystic Julian of Norwich, "all shall be well and all shall be well and all manner of thing shall be well." The understanding of God as a non-coercive force of inviting love that was developed in chapter three of this book and is advocated by many theologians today prevents one from arguing *on the basis of the empirical observation of secondary causes* that all will certainly "be well" in the long run. A key strength of the primary-secondary distinction is that secondary causes are granted a genuine efficacy of their own. As Peacocke said in his address accepting the prestigious Templeton Prize for Progress in Religion, "God endows the world with its own autonomy to function according to its God-given relationships, . . . God works in, with and under what we call the 'natural' processes of the world and does not coerce but invites the co-operation of humanity in the divine creative process shaping the world and human life."[45] Accordingly, it cannot readily be assumed that the behavior of humans or other intelligent beings will always be in accord with divine intent; otherwise, freely chosen evil deeds would be non-existent. Strictly speaking, one cannot *know* that God's providential guidance will ultimately prevail, though the conviction that it will is certainly an essential aspect of Judeo-Christian and Islamic belief.

In general, this approach of Aquinas, Farrer, and Johnson seems to me more satisfactory than those of the authors described earlier in this chapter. It fully acknowledges the agency of secondary causes, which can be examined by the methodologically naturalistic procedures of natural science without in any way impugning the primary causality of God as accepted on faith by religious believers. There is, however, one final issue that must be addressed in this connection, that of the "extraordinary" activity of the miraculous. Claims of miraculous occurrences are found in religious traditions throughout the world. Within mainstream Christianity, Aquinas taught that when God chooses, God can produce effects directly, without secondary causes, and these things that God does "outside those causes which we know, are called miracles."[46] What, then, of miracles? How are they to be understood, and what questions do they raise about divine action?

A Note on Miracles

In modern times, the notion of miracle regularly presupposes a conception of "nature" as a closed system of laws that is somehow "broken" by a direct intervention of God. Scripture scholars regularly point out there was no such presupposition in biblical times. The Israelites saw the world around them as exhibiting the constant activity of God, and the authors of the New Testament likewise show little or no understanding of nature as a systematic unity governed by fixed laws of causality. Nevertheless, certain occurrences were understood by the biblical authors to stand out from the normal course of events. The wonderful deeds worked by Jesus are normally called *dynameis* ("works of power") or *semeia* ("signs"), though there are warnings in the New Testament that one should not go about seeking such phenomena, as when

Jesus answers a request from the scribes and Pharisees with the rebuke: "An evil and adulterous generation seeks for a sign, but no sign shall be given to it except the sign of the prophet Jonah" (Matt 12:39). On the other hand, there are clear affirmations, especially in the Fourth Gospel, that the signs worked by Jesus were previously unheard of and therefore manifested divine action in a special way. Thus, the account of the restoration of sight to the man born blind includes the latter's words: "Never since the world began has it been heard that anyone opened the eyes of a man born blind. If this man were not from God, he could do nothing" (Jn. 9:32–33). Even though the apologetic use of miracles became more prominent in later Church history, as when the First Vatican Council affirmed that miracles could be used to prove the divine origin of the Christian religion, there was already an apologetic element in the Johannine passage quoted above and in similar ones. When the very existence of miracles came to be severely questioned in recent centuries, as in the works of Spinoza and Hume and of more recent authors like Anthony Flew and Bertrand Russell, Christian thinkers naturally felt obliged to respond. My present discussion of the issue will focus on the way this response has been formulated within the context of the dialogue between science and religion.

Back in chapter one we saw that Schleiermacher considered even the most natural and common event to be miraculous as soon as the religious view of it became dominant, to such an extent that for a truly religious person "all is miracle." This "liberal" understanding of miracle is not what is under discussion in the science-religion dialogue, but rather what the New Testament scholar John Meier has defined as "(1) an unusual, startling, or extraordinary event that is in principle perceivable by an interested and fair-minded observer, (2) an event that finds no reasonable explanation in human abilities or in other known forces that operate in our world of time and space, and (3) an event that is the result of a special act of God, doing what no human power can do."[47] The fact that such an event is, by definition, unusual means that not every single person will directly experience one even in the course of a lifetime but will have to rely on reports of others and make critical judgments about their authenticity and freedom from error. Having read accounts of miracles by authors like the Nobel Prize-winning medical doctor Alexis Carrel and the theologian Louis Monden,[48] I myself have no doubt that the first two parts of Meier's definition of miracle are reasonably verifiable, though I recognize that someone who considers miracles impossible *a priori* will question even such reports. I also recognize that the third aspect of Meier's definition — that the event is the result of a special act of God — is not open to a convincing demonstration by the methods of natural science, whose methodological naturalism prevents it from demonstrating the existence of any reality transcending the spatio-temporal order. As one scientist has written, "in all my training in science, there was never any mention of even the possibility that anything other than natural causes should be included in scientific explanations."[49] A religious believer certainly need not be disturbed by such an avowal, which simply means that, confronted with such an event, a scientist *as such* can only say that no natural explanation seems possible, though he or she might hold out the hope that such an explanation will one day be available.

It should also be noted, however, that many scientists, and certainly all mainstream theologians, are convinced that science is not our only valid avenue to a genuine understanding of reality. In the careful studies of allegedly miraculous phenomena that I have read — especially accounts of the healing of organic diseases — the investigators found indications (though not strict proofs) that there were factors at work that were not detectable by empirical investigation. Monden, for example, writes that prayer is the only invariable factor present in all of the miraculous cures that he studied. In his words, "this prayer may be full of confidence, or weakened by doubting and vacillation; it may be simple as that of a child, or virile and direct as the prayer of a grown man; hesitant upon the lips of the atheist or unbeliever, but piercing when uttered by a mother who is prepared to reap the gift of heaven by violence,"[50] but it is in any case the one constant. To claim that this somehow proves God's direct activity would itself be a statement of faith, but a religious person can readily affirm this, since faith is doctrinally considered a gift and, in the words of the Christian philosopher Diogenes Allen, one must first have this gift "in order to be in a position to recognize the manifestation of divine activity in nature, history, and individual lives."[51]

It therefore ought not be at all problematic for a believing Christian (or Jew or Muslim or other theist) to admit that we cannot point to action by God with the same kind of empirical clarity that is available in a scientific laboratory, for there are ineluctable limitations on our ability to comprehend what it would mean to be a divine agent. There is even something radically liberating about this admission, for it can free one from that hankering after signs that Jesus condemned in Matthew's Gospel. A person may be a devout believer and yet feel very uneasy when reading about the large crowds that seem regularly to converge upon the site of this or that supposedly miraculous apparition, whether in Lubbock, Texas, or Conyers, Georgia, or elsewhere. Much more in keeping with the cautious attitude of my own Catholic tradition was the attitude of the sixteenth-century mystic and Doctor of the Church St. John of the Cross, who would refuse to join others who wanted to go to some nearby site to behold someone with allegedly miraculous powers. His own position was that if God was truly and directly at work in such a person, then good would come of it without a crowd of spectators looking on, whereas if the activity was not from God, those in attendance would only be misled and spiritually harmed. He accordingly wrote that "God is not inclined to work miracles.... [Christ] reprimanded the Pharisees because they would not give assent without signs: *If you do not see signs and wonders, you do not believe* [Jn. 4:48].... The more the soul believes in and serves God without testimonies and signs, the more it extols God, since it believes more of him than signs and miracles can teach."[52] Relying on the miraculous can even be judged to go against what a contemporary Jewish author calls "the order of creation." Without at all denying the possibility and possible helpfulness of miraculous divine interventions (a theist could hardly deny this possibility absolutely), Eliezer Shore wisely advises that we should look in another direction for long-term growth: Real change regularly comes "from below, born out of our struggles and aspirations.... Though it may be less dramatic than a miracle, the transformation it effects is permanent. Furthermore, by acknowledging those areas in our lives that need improvement and by working to repair the broken pieces of both self and world, we must, of necessity, involve everything around us in the process, and thereby refine and uplift the world. This is not a 'moment of grace' but a complete reintegration of every aspect of life."[53] Among the aspects of life that can thereby be brought to an ever-fuller, mutual integration are precisely the disciplines of natural science and theology.

7

Essaying Coherence

A S NOTED in the preface to this book, my primary purpose has been to explore the implications of certain central findings of natural science for traditional theological doctrines. A number of these implications have been considered in each of the preceding chapters. Rather than merely summarize points already made, this final chapter will be *an essay* in the literal sense of the term, that is, an attempt to build on observations made earlier in this book and so to present a coherent understanding of some fundamental theological notions in the light of what modern science has told us about the world in which we live, including ourselves as part of this world. In the past, theologians were sometimes so intent on reflecting on the relationship between human beings and God that the rest of creation was relatively ignored. This will no longer do, especially because of the continuity that science reveals between humans and other living beings and between all of these and the larger inanimate world in which they exist. The three principal topics of this final chapter will accordingly be God, human beings, and the rest of creation, none of these understood simply in themselves but in their various interrelationships. Even though countless books and articles have been published about each of these topics, I hope that the following reflections will shed new light on what are among the most central realities for religious persons.

God

Toward the end of chapter one I quoted Karl Rahner to the effect that our contemporary awareness of the awesome size of the

133

universe and of the way this can heighten a sense of God's immensity and infinite qualitative difference from us brings with it
a danger: theologians and other academics face the temptation
of suppressing this realization "in a hasty and cheap apologetic
for an anthropomorphic 'belief in God.' "[1] Rahner and the many
other modern theologians who have regularly emphasized the mysterious nature of divine reality, even to the point of privileging
"Absolute Mystery" as the divine name *par excellence,* will certainly not be suspected of inappropriately anthropomorphizing
God. There is, however, one crucial point on which he and other
mainstream theologians have always insisted, namely, that God is
truly personal, even if this term can be used of God only analogously on the basis of what we know of human persons. In a
forceful response to an interviewer who once asked him if it might
not be possible to be religious in a certain sense and yet ignore
the question of God, Rahner replied: "If God is only interesting
to me as a stopgap and guarantor of my 'needs,' then I am not
speaking of the true God. The true God is the God who must
be worshiped and loved for his own sake. He is the enormous
and radical, all-supporting and penetrating reality of the most personal kind, toward which I must direct myself and to which I must
surrender myself."[2]

With this position I am in total agreement. Indeed, it is difficult to see how theologians could go beyond this and still be
considered orthodox. However, it is important to note that some
have gone further, precisely because of their sense of the theological implications of modern science. Perhaps the best-known
exemplar of this more radical position, at least in North America,
is Gordon Kaufman, emeritus professor at the Harvard Divinity
School. Elaborating on a stance he took in his book *In Face of
Mystery* (1993), he recently wrote: "As far as we know, personal
agential beings did not exist, and *could not have existed,* before
billions of years of cosmic evolution of a very specific sort and
then further billions of years of biological evolution also of a very
specific sort had transpired. How, then, can we today think of
a person-like creator-God as existing before and apart from any

such evolutionary developments?"[3] In place of "creator," a notion he rejects as being unacceptably anthropomorphic, Kaufman speaks of "creativity," which he understands as "very close to being a synonym of the concept of mystery," differing only in that creativity "directs attention to the coming into being of the new."[4] Practically speaking, this means that for him "the childlike trust, assurance, and consolation characteristic of the conviction that throughout our lives we are cared for lovingly by a heavenly father are no longer available," even though Kaufman does claim that "serendipitous creativity" can itself be worshiped and, indeed, is "the *sole* appropriate focus for human devotion and worship."[5]

Kaufman is a serious thinker who has dealt with the question of God throughout his scholarly career, so it would be altogether out of place to make light of the position that he advocates. His conclusions do not, however, follow logically from the findings of evolutionary science. To say that personal agential beings "could not have existed" before billions of years of cosmic and biological evolution is self-evident if one is referring only to beings that have come into existence on the face of the earth, but mainstream theology in all of the major theistic traditions has so emphatically understood God as distinct from the individual beings that have evolved on earth that it is difficult to see how Kaufman's argument could really be convincing. In terms of a distinction I have made at several places in this book, he not only tries to make his theology coherent with modern science but in fact conflates the two branches of knowledge. This comes across with particular clarity when Kaufman writes, in criticism of John Polkinghorne, that to take seriously "all that science tells us about the workings of the world" means acknowledging a "*central* scientific understanding: that complex features of the world such as conscious intention, purposive action, deliberate creation of artifacts, loving attitudes and behaviors, and the like... can come into being only *after* billions of years of complex cosmic, biological, and historical development have provided the necessary conditions for their emergence to occur."[6] This argument based on "what science tells us" is cogent only to the extent that one's purview is limited to the spatio-temporal realm of beings that are amenable to investigation by the empirical methods of natural science. To go beyond this and conclude, as Kaufman does, that this necessarily rules out the existence of God as traditionally understood in the Judeo-Christian and other theistic traditions is a clear example of scientism and should be recognized as such. That many persons agree with Kaufman's position, even though they may not be able to express it as fluently as he, is an indication of the extent to which scientism characterizes much of contemporary consciousness.

Recognizing the logical shortcomings of that position does not, however, mean that a traditional understanding of what Rahner called a God "of the most personal kind" is without its own challenges. In the part of this book dealing with the question of an *anima separata,* we have seen Rahner claiming that modern metaphysical anthropology can scarcely argue for the possibility of "an absolutely non-material mode of existence on the part of the spiritual subject." But it is this very point about the existence of a non-material, unembodied reality that — when transferred from the discipline of metaphysical anthropology to theology (or to the philosophy of God) — has been problematic for many persons past and present. One of the major turning points in that quintessential conversion story, Augustine's *Confessions,* is his account of how, after years of questioning and finally with the help of Platonic philosophy, he came to accept the existence of purely spiritual reality. In book five he laments: "When I tried to think of my God, I could think of him only as a bodily substance, because I could not conceive of the existence of anything else. This was the principal and almost the only cause of the error from which I could not escape."[7] Later, through the good offices of a man whom Augustine does not name, he procured Latin translations of Greek treatises written by the Platonic (we would say Neoplatonic) philosophers Plotinus, Porphyry, Iamblichus, and Proclus. The effect of these works on him was monumental, for "by reading these books of the Platonists I had been prompted to look for truth as something incorporeal, and I 'caught sight of your invisible nature, as it is known through your creatures' [Rom. 1:20]. . . . I was certain both that you are and that you are infinite, though without extent in terms of space either limited or unlimited. . . . I knew too that all other things derive their being from you, and the one indisputable proof of this is the fact that they exist at all."[8]

There may be no other passage in Western Christian literature that offers so personal and clear an affirmation of the spiritual nature of divine reality as distinct from and transcending the limits of the spatio-temporal world. Even though one cannot strictly imagine what such a reality is like, one can reasonably affirm God's existence as the ultimate answer to the question of why there is anything rather than nothing, what Keith Ward has called "the completion of that search for intelligibility which characterizes the scientific enterprise."[9] If and when this distinction between God and the world is affirmed in so one-sided a way that God's immanence is ignored or understated, one ends up with a particular form of "classical theism" against which Philip Clayton and other panentheists protest. There is, however, really no need to insist on a stark dichotomy between theism and panentheism, for at its best classical theism has affirmed God's immanence without derogating from the note of transcendence. In Augustine this is sometimes expressed in memorable phraseology: on the one hand, he asks of the transcendent God, "Can even heaven and earth, which you made and in which you made me, contain you?" while on the other hand he famously laments, "Late have I learned to love you, O Beauty at once so ancient and so new! Late have I learned to love you! You were within me, and I was in the world outside myself."[10]

This kind of dialectical polarity is inescapable if one wishes to present an adequately full understanding of God. As John Macquarrie has written, the terms "transcendence" and "immanence" are not to be taken as "destructive contradictions or even sheer paradoxes" but rather as pointers to the fullness of divine reality understood as being in some respects wholly transcendent and in some respects entirely immanent.[11] For anyone who is satisfied with the search for explanations given in the form of empirical observations and principles, the position represented by theists like Augustine and Macquarrie will, of course, not be of much interest and may even appear fundamentally misguided. The physicist Steven Weinberg, already mentioned several times in this book, recently published a paper dealing with the concept of explanation in the natural sciences. He there expressed the hope that "in the future we will have achieved an understanding of all the regularities that we see in nature, based on a few simple principles, laws of nature [such as Newton's law of gravitation or Einstein's theory of general relativity], from which all other regularities can be deduced."[12] This does indeed refer to one sort of explanation, but it is quite different from that adduced in the discipline of theology. The latter seeks to elucidate what is experienced, in faith, of God as both the transcendent origin and ground of the universe and also the immanent presence in the inmost core of all that is. The scriptures of every major theistic tradition express this in one way or another. The New Testament, for example, speaks of a triune God who has not only created all that is but who also abides in each believer, as when in the Fourth Gospel Jesus promises, "Whoever loves me will keep my word, and my Father will love him, and we will come to him and make our dwelling with him" (Jn. 14:23). So, too, the Qur'an, which not only exalts God as the omnipotent and omniscient Lord of all but also as intimately present to each human being: "We created man. We know the promptings of his soul, and are closer to him than the vein of his neck."[13] Within the Hindu tradition, one of the most commonly quoted sayings from the Upanishads and other religious literature of India refers to the ultimate identity between Brahman and Atman, that is, between the infinite source of everything and the universal self at the heart of each being. I refer to such passages not as proof texts but rather as pointers to two aspects of the divine that must both be affirmed in order to do justice to the widespread experience of God in all parts of the world. Such experience does indeed go beyond—but is not incompatible with—what the natural sciences can detect.

Likewise going beyond but not contradicting empirical observation is what the major theistic traditions say about love as especially characteristic of God's being. The centrality of love in these traditions was noted in chapter three. To be sure, dwelling on this point entails the danger of overly romanticizing one's concept of God; Rudolf Otto's emphasis on the divine as a mystery that is not only attractive but also awesome and even frightening, a *mysterium tremendum et fascinans*, must not be forgotten.[14] If, however, we follow Karl Schmitz-Moormann in understanding divine love as not only a moral but also an ontological reality, what he called "the driving force of the evolutionary process of progressing union,"[15] sentimentality may be avoided and a theological or metaphysical explanation be made available for the trajectory toward increasing complexity that is evident in the story of evolution. Drawing upon process thought in the tradition of Alfred North Whitehead and Charles Hartshorne, one can add the note of non-coerciveness to this understanding of God's love. If, at the human level, love at its best respects the freedom of the other and is for that reason liberating rather than dominating, then divine love can similarly be understood as persuasive, respecting the freedom of creatures "to be themselves" and so to respond to the divine allurement in positive ways without forcing such responses upon them. Only with some such understanding of divine reality can one avoid the charge of making God a kind of transcendent puppeteer. This likewise leaves an opening for that element of genuine chance so central in contemporary evolutionary theory, allowing this element to be affirmed rather than denied by religious persons.

If we do not conceive of God as determining all the details of worldly occurrences but instead respecting the genuine efficacy of secondary causes, there still remains the question of whether God ever acts in this world in a way that bypasses such causes. As noted in my treatment of miracles in the preceding chapter, this possibility has been denied by various thinkers in recent centuries. In addition to persons mentioned in that chapter (such as Spinoza, Hume, and Bertrand Russell), one could add the name of Albert Einstein. In an article on the relationship between religion and science published in 1930, this great scientist argued that anyone "who is thoroughly convinced of the universal operation of the law of causation cannot for a moment entertain the idea of a being who interferes in the course of events — provided, of course, that he takes the hypothesis of causality really seriously."[16] One may certainly admire Einstein for stating the issue so simply and clearly. If one takes the hypothesis "really seriously," meaning that if one assumes *a priori* that the spatio-temporal order constitutes a web that can never be broken, then divine interference of this sort is certainly inadmissible. I have already noted in the preceding chapter that one could not, on scientific grounds, prove that an apparently inexplicable event could never in the future receive a satisfactory explanation on an empirical level. One could, of course, retain the notion of miracle by following Schleiermacher and defining it as *any* event viewed from a religious perspective. Then, indeed, one could say that "all is miracle." There is an attractive consistency to this position, which likewise countermands that search for special signs and wonders against which Jesus himself inveighed. Some might even argue that one could not practice science in a credible way without being convinced of what Einstein called "the universal operation of the law of causation."

Without making the possibility of what Einstein called "divine interference" a linchpin of one's theology, it nevertheless seems to me that one could reasonably leave open the real possibility that at times, and for reasons unfathomable to us, a loving God could directly bring about some occurrences that could not, in principle, be explained by the methods of natural science. It goes without saying that some events in the past were too readily proclaimed as miraculous when natural explanations later became available, so a certain degree of caution and even skepticism is definitely called for in such matters. Nevertheless, there have been documented healings in religious contexts that, in the words of the Oxford professor of modern history Ruth Harris, show "the limits of historical explanation" and thereby "dismay and perplex" those whose worldview has no possible place for such phenomena.[17] When the medical doctor Alexis Carrel wrote a short book about one such healing that he had himself observed, most of his secular colleagues in France condemned him so strongly for his "betrayal" that he emigrated to the United States, where he eventually became a Nobel laureate. Carrel considered it part of his scientific mission to show "a willingness to entertain new possibilities, to question the reigning positivism of the previous generation."[18] This kind of openmindedness, avoiding the extremes of both the thoroughly skeptical and the naively gullible, has a strong claim to our allegiance still today. For a religious person, such "new possibilities" would comprise one part of an overall attitude of reverence that accepts not only the ultimate incomprehensibility of God but also our inability to fit everything that happens or could happen into the confines of explanations available within the disciplines of the historical or the natural sciences. No religious author has expressed this attitude more poignantly than St. Paul when he exclaimed in his Letter to the Romans: "O the depth of the riches and wisdom and knowledge of God! How unsearchable are his judgments and how inscrutable his ways! 'For who has known the mind of the Lord, or who has been his counselor?'" (Rom. 11:33–34). When Paul wrote those words he had one particular issue in mind (the Jews and Gentiles in God's providence), but they are just as applicable to the entire range of religious encounter with God. As will be noted in the next section of this chapter, there is an ineluctably mysterious character to human beings as well.

Human Beings

Natural science, as such, cannot investigate divine reality, but it rightly has much to say about human beings, as do certain branches of theology, especially that known as theological anthropology. In keeping with the overall purpose of this book, I will here reflect on a few implications of modern science for a theological understanding of the human person. For some scientists, the primary implication is that theology has nothing relevant to say for the simple reason that human beings are viewed as being no more than complex machines. This may be minority view even within the scientific arena, but it was voiced with forceful conviction by the prestigious French biologist Jacques Monod, who wrote in one of his best-known books that "man knows at last that he is alone in the universe's unfeeling immensity, out of which he

emerged only by chance."[19] Monod followed up that statement in
a lecture broadcast by the BBC, when he claimed that "anything
can be reduced to simple, obvious mechanical interactions. The
cell is a machine. The animal is a machine. Man is a machine."[20]
If one accepts this thoroughly reductionistic view of human reality,
then a scientist's main challenge will be to analyze the component
parts of this machine so completely as to explain their interaction
in a deterministic way. Biologists following the lead of Monod and
psychiatrists who are strict disciples of Freud take this approach.
If the term "mystery" is applicable at all here, it is only in the
secondary sense of a complicated problem that might eventually
be solved after diligent investigation. There is, of course, little or
no possibility of fruitful theological dialogue with scientists who
adamantly hold this position.

A different set of challenges arises out of evolutionary theory.
We have already seen in chapter three that the element of random-
ness or chance within this theory is not at all an insurmountable
problem for theologians, provided they do not take divine providence to imply a design divinely ordered in all its details. If God
is the source of genuine novelty and even of what could be called
"creative disorder," then one would actually expect to find the
incredibly variegated forms of life that paleontology has discovered from the past and that biologists study in the living world
today. What may seem problematic is the implication that human
beings are not necessarily the unsurpassable pinnacle of all forms
of life. Because humans have now spread to all parts of the earth,
the relative lack of geographical isolation that has regularly been
a necessary condition for macro-evolutionary change may indeed
make it unlikely — though not impossible — that our species will
evolve on earth in any significant way. But it is quite possible that
in future centuries or millennia space travel could provide the degree of isolation requisite for the emergence of a new species,
even though one could not predict this with any degree of certainty at the present time. The mere possibility of imagining such
a development, however, should lead to an appropriate degree of
humility far removed from those utterances and attitudes of in-

vincible human superiority that characterized many of our race in previous generations. We simply have no way of knowing what biological developments lie in the distant future, when even the near-term future may hold unimaginable surprises.

Moreover, when one considers the hundreds of thousands of years during which *Homo sapiens* has existed on earth and contrasts that vast time span with the relatively few thousand years in which our current political, social, and religious traditions have developed, it is incumbent upon us to value the latter for the guidance they can surely provide but not to regard them as relatively immune to change. Just as development has characterized the biological story of life as this has been investigated by the life sciences, so too has development characterized the human traditions that have emerged. Continuity and discontinuity, sameness and difference mark all of our traditions, including the religious and the theological, as John Henry Newman showed in his magisterial *Essay on the Development of Christian Doctrine* (1845). Considering that the city in which I live, Washington, D.C., did not even exist when the American colonies declared their independence as recently as the late eighteenth century, it would be an exercise in futility to try to imagine what cultural life on this part of the planet will look like a thousand or ten thousand years from now, not to mention a million years. So, too, when one ponders the developments in the Christian church's practice and doctrine over the past two millennia, it would be useless to try to depict in any detail the course of these developments two millennia or twenty millennia hence. To be part of the ongoing stream of life and to participate in its flow, whether as a scientist or a theologian, is a bracing but humbling privilege, potentially a source of great joy *and* great consternation. It is fitting to seek as much knowledge about human reality as possible, but the unavoidable limits set by our ignorance about future developments is one of the reasons why we must ascribe to humanity the same note of mystery that properly and even more fittingly belongs to God. Karl Rahner expressed this with forthright conviction when he once said in an interview:

We cannot adequately explain the essence of the human person. That is, we cannot rationally reduce this essence to one element whose composition then defines the whole person. A human person necessarily always remains a mystery, and in the act of her freedom — a freedom that psychologists must not deny — a person must entrust herself, a mystery, to the absolute mystery of God, who is loving, trustworthy, and forgiving.[21]

One further kind of trust is equally necessary — a trust of one's fellow human beings. Genocidal events of the past century offer plenty of reasons to be wary of others, whose surface civility may mask vast reservoirs of potential cruelty. Suspicion, however, has never been the primary characteristic of persons like Gandhi and Mother Teresa, whom we recognize as having done so much to foster a world in which centripetal forces outstrip the centrifugal. Teilhard de Chardin often referred to the kind of uncertainty facing our race because of tension between forces of isolation and repulsion driving humans apart (as occurred in recent times in places like Rwanda and the former Yugoslavia) and forces drawing them together. Even the forces tending toward unification are of very distinct kinds, not all of them desirable. As Teilhard observed, one sort of unity arises merely from forces of external pressure and compulsion, such as unrestrained population growth or the constraints imposed by a stronger group upon a weaker. Ultimately this cannot satisfy, for "unification through coercion leads only to a superficial pseudo-unity. It may establish a mechanism, but it does not achieve any fundamental synthesis, and in consequence it engenders no growth of consciousness. It materializes, in short, instead of spiritualizing."[22] The alternative is the way of love — universal, mutual love. There are vast possibilities for self-deception here, whether on the part of civic or religious leaders or of individuals, for the temptation to control or possess the one(s) allegedly loved will regularly be present. Courage and ruthless honesty are indispensable, as is the recognition that it is just as important to be willing to receive love and support from another as it is to offer these to persons in need. On a personal level this was described in a particularly vivid way some years ago by a woman named Stephani Cook, who had suffered an almost unimaginable series of medical misdiagnoses that had left her on the point of death. Looking back on this painful period of her life spent in a New York hospital, she recalled how important it was, for herself and others, simply to let herself be loved when she could do nothing more:

> My friends sustain me, each in a singular and loving way; my sister comes down from Boston almost every weekend to be near. There are times when I can't be amusing or even amused, times when I am too sick to do anything but lie here with my eyes closed, and still they come to sit wordlessly by the bed and hold my hand, keeping me company through the long hours.
>
> Because we go through this together, I learn as much about myself as I do about them. I learn something about the more positive aspects of dependence, learn that allowing somebody else to assume the major responsibility of caring and loving is not the same as taking without giving anything back. My friends need to be supportive as I need to be sick, and when I stop interpreting our intercourse in a manner consistent with an ordinary-use model, I have stunningly powerful experiences of intimacy and sharing.[23]

Stephani Cook was not, of course, writing anything like a traditional scientific treatise when she composed those memoirs, but what she came to understand is very much in accord with what we can learn from both the social and the natural sciences. Particle physics reveals that even at the subatomic level entities are simultaneously influencing others and being influenced by them, though not always in the same proportion. What is true there is just as true at all other levels of reality, including human life on both the social and the individual plane. At that particular time in Stephani Cook's life, the most healthful thing she could do for herself and her family and friends was to let them love and support her, whereas upon her recovery she was able to take a far more active role in her relationship with others. This illustrates one of the qualities most needed in some societies today, especially parts of the world where longstanding animosities have led to decades of almost unrelenting violence and mistrust. There are no easy answers to something like the ongoing conflict between Israelis and Palestinians, but what is surely needed by persons on both sides of such disputes is a truthful, courageous admission that at times a society may be too sick to help itself and can recover only by trusting responsible persons from outside the group to offer the procedures and policies necessary for healing, it being taken for granted that substantial compromise will be needed on the part of all concerned. Because of the above-mentioned mystery characterizing each human being (and hence each human society), activity in such areas can never be as predictable as it might be when one is dealing with relatively simple elements in a physics laboratory. The overall parallelism does, however, seem to be an absolutely crucial aspect of one's view of the world if, in Schmitz-Moormann's words, one understands love to be fundamental — and not simply as a moral force but one that arises from the very nature of reality, "the constitutive force, the driving force of the evolutionary process of progressing union."[24] This may be the most significant insight that science can offer us in our attempts to foster a genuine civilization of love. The next and last section of this book will extend these insights to the way we humans relate to the rest of creation.

Other Beings

Some decades ago the greatest threat to the continued existence of the human race was widely considered to be nuclear warfare. No thinking person today will minimize this danger, but in more recent times the focus of concern has shifted more and more to the environment. The loss of biodiversity that accompanies the gradual destruction of the tropical rain forests, the superficially comical but potentially tragic stories one hears about misguided attempts to dispose safely of hazardous waste, and our world's countless cases of infant mortality due to inadequate nutrition and hygiene are just three of the ways in which environmental issues have reached crisis or near-crisis levels. Some environmentalists caution against entrusting the finding of solutions to scientists and technicians on the grounds that we can never know the long-term results of human intervention and so may do more harm than good,[25] but a reasonable alternative is to make use of whatever scientific knowledge is available to us but to do so with a sense of kinship with and reverence for the rest of creation. This latter point is crucial. The Greek Orthodox theologian John Chryssavgis has argued convincingly that our current way of life "is humanly and environmentally suicidal. Unless we change it radically, we cannot hope to avoid or reverse cosmic catastrophe."[26] The crisis, he continues, concerns "the way we perceive, imagine, image. We are treating our environment, our planet, in an inhuman, god-forsaken manner," which means that the root of the problem is ultimately religious and that the response "must also be religious, even if the results will be evident in our economy and [system of] justice, in our policy and politics, in our technology and science."[27]

For all the criticism that the Judeo-Christian tradition has received from Lynn White and his disciples, there are also vast resources for ecological healing within this tradition, especially if its adherents act in accordance with key findings of modern science. In chapter three I pointed out that one of the most significant conclusions to be drawn from the recent mapping of the human genetic code is that we are genetically kin not only to every other human being but also to every living entity on earth, past or present. What St. Francis understood instinctively in his practice of addressing other creatures as his brothers and sisters has now been given a firm scientific foundation. A practical corollary is that if and when we must in some way harm or even kill another creature, as for purposes of nutrition or medical research, we ought do so with reverent reluctance. Members of religious traditions who are even more stringent in this regard, such as Jains who take precautions to avoid even accidentally killing an insect, will perhaps never be literally imitated by many others, but they at least do the rest of us the great service of helping inculcate a sense of reverence for all life. Classic thinkers within the Christian tradition point us in the same direction. Thus John Calvin, referring to the God-given book of nature as complementing the book of scripture, inveighed against the senseless killing of a parent bird tending its young in the following words: "If we burn the book which our Lord has shown us, wittingly undermining the order he has established in nature by playing the butcher in killing the defenseless bird with our own hands — if we thereby prevent the bird from discharging its fatherly or motherly duty, then what will become of us?"[28] Closer to our own time, Jürgen Moltmann has expressed the interconnectedness of the whole natural world in a more general way. Working out of an explicitly Trinitarian context but in terms that many members of other religious traditions should find acceptable, he writes: "If the Holy Spirit is poured out on the whole creation, then [the Spirit] creates the community of all created things with God and with each other, making it that fellowship of creation in which all created things communicate with one another and with God, each in its own way."[29]

If one takes seriously the reality of this interconnectedness, it cannot but affect the way we relate to the world around us. To the possible objection that the responsible actions of one individual or small group could have little impact in a world where environmental problems are so enormous, the only proper response is that we should each gladly do whatever we can, trusting that our actions will influence others but acting in an ecologically sensitive way regardless. An anecdote recounted by the author of a popular work in the field of eco-spirituality exemplifies this attitude, one that is both scientifically informed and personally fulfilling. Speaking of a family in the northwestern United States who resolved to invest in the equipment necessary to provide their own electricity through solar energy, Charles Cummings writes that the best this family can expect economically is to break even. Nevertheless they have taken this step because "they are committed to eco-spiritual living. In this way they are leading by example, proclaiming their values for others to notice and perhaps follow. Even if no one should imitate them, they have the satisfaction of living according to their convictions and of knowing that their contribution does help."[30]

A central conviction underlying such behavior — the interconnectedness of all reality — is consonant with both the findings of modern science and the tenets of many religious traditions. Knowing that the very elements that compose our bodies were forged eons ago in the depths of distant stars and then spewed forth in gigantic supernovae explosions cannot but impress upon our consciousness a definite sense of kinship with the cosmos as a whole. Again, knowing that paleontology, genetics, and other sciences have revealed our genealogical communion with all other living things on earth cannot but make us more keenly aware of a genuine relationship to these and of an obligation to avoid senselessly destructive behavior toward them. These and other findings from the scientific arena can in turn be complemented by the example of classic figures from the world's religions. To refer one final time to the saint who is best known in this regard in the West, Francis of Assisi clearly offers us what we have seen Paul Santmire call "the rudiments for a theology that has ... a special vocabulary for nature, the vocabulary of friendship; that envisions a close ontological bond between God and humans, on the one hand, and nature, on the other; that presupposes an understanding of God that readily highlights those qualities of the divine life that show God as immanent in and as befriending all creatures and that, accordingly, encourages humans to do the same."[31] To the extent that we are willing to "do the same," the dialogue between science and theology that has been explored throughout this book may not only open up new avenues for theoretical reflection but also help promote a more integrated and healthful way of life for us as individuals, as members of our larger human societies, as brothers and sisters of all other living beings, and as creatures responding in a positive way to the alluring love of God.

Notes

Preface

1. Ian Barbour, *Religion and Science: Historical and Contemporary Issues* (San Francisco: Harper, 1997), xiii.

2. "Message of His Holiness Pope John Paul II," in *Physics, Philosophy, and Theology: A Common Quest for Understanding,* ed. Robert J. Russell et al., 3rd ed. (Vatican City State: Vatican Observatory, 1997), M10.

I. Historical Background

1. Michael Behe, *Darwin's Black Box* (New York: The Free Press, 1996); Philip E. Johnson, *Darwin on Trial* (Washington, D.C.: Regnery Gateway, 1991).

2. Kenneth R. Miller, *Finding Darwin's God: A Scientist's Search for Common Ground between God and Evolution* (New York: Cliff Street Books, 1999); John F. Haught, *God after Darwin: A Theology of Evolution* (Boulder: Westview Press, 2000).

3. Leonardo da Vinci, quoted in Peter Burke, *Tradition and Innovation in Renaissance Italy* (London, 1974), 208.

4. Johannes Kepler, quoted in Robert S. Westman, "Magical Reform and Astronomical Reform: The Yates Thesis Reconsidered," in *Hermeticism and the Scientific Revolution,* by Robert S. Westman and J. E. McGuire (Los Angeles: William Andrews Clark Memorial Library, University of California, 1977), 41.

5. John Hedley Brooke, *Science and Religion: Some Historical Perspectives* (Cambridge: Cambridge University Press, 1991), 121.

6. Francis Bacon, "Of Atheism," in idem, *Essays, Advancement of Learning, New Atlantis, and Other Pieces,* ed. Richard Foster Jones (New York: Odyssey, 1937), 47.

7. *Theological Works of the Hon. Robert Boyle,* prefixed by his Life by Richard Boulton, 3 vols. (London, 1715).

8. Boyle, *A Free Inquiry into the Vulgarly Received Notion of Nature,* quoted by Richard S. Westfall, *Science and Religion in Seventeenth-Century England* (New Haven: Yale University Press, 1958), 70.

9. *The Works of the Honourable Robert Boyle,* ed. Thomas Birch (London, 1772), 5:162.

10. Kenelm Digby, *Observations upon Religio Medici,* published with Browne's *Religio Medici* (Oxford: Clarendon Press, 1909), 10.

11. Nehemiah Grew, *Cosmologia Sacra,* quoted by Westfall, *Science and Religion,* 100.

12. Isaac Newton, *Mathematical Principles of Natural Philosophy,* trans. Andrew Motte, revised by Florian Cajori, in *Newton, Huygens,* vol. 34 of Great Books of the Western World (Chicago: Encyclopaedia Britannica, 1952), 369–70.

13. Westfall, *Science and Religion,* 92.

14. John Dillenberger, *Protestant Thought and Natural Science: A Historical Interpretation* (Notre Dame, Ind.: University of Notre Dame Press, 1988), 189.

15. Schleiermacher, "Zweites Sendschreiben an Herrn Dr. Lücke," in idem, *Sämtliche Werke,* Erste Abtheilung, *Zur Theologie* (Berlin: G. Reimer, 1836), 2:613.

16. On this point, see Martin Redeker, *Schleiermacher: Life and Thought,* trans. John Wallhausser (Philadelphia: Fortress Press, 1973), 119. Redeker writes earlier in his book: "He [Schleiermacher] was particularly concerned with the changes brought on by the devastation of supernaturalistic metaphysics in the wake of modern science and Kant's critical philosophy. Even so,...he was confident that the gospel would be rediscovered and authenticated in a new way" (2).

17. Schleiermacher, *The Christian Faith,* 2nd ed., ed. H. R. Mackintosh and J. S. Stewart (Edinburgh: T&T Clark, 1989), 174 (sec. 46.2). My emphasis. In a footnote, Schleiermacher referred to a leading theologian of Lutheran orthodoxy, Johann Andreas Quenstedt, who argued in his *Systema Theologicum* that one and the same event was to be seen as dependent "a Deo ut causa universali, a creatura ut particulari."

18. Louis Dupré, "Schleiermacher's Religion as Feeling," in idem, *A Dubious Heritage: Studies in the Philosophy of Religion after Kant* (New York: Paulist Press, 1977), 22.

19. Schleiermacher, *The Christian Faith,* 170–71 (sec. 46.1).

20. Ibid., 171.

21. Ibid., 172.

22. Redeker, *Schleiermacher,* 120.

23. Schleiermacher, *On Religion,* trans. John Oman (New York: Harper, Torch Books, 1958), 88.

24. Schleiermacher, *The Christian Faith,* 183 (sec. 47.3).

25. Ibid., 180 (sec. 47.1).

26. Karl Barth, "Concluding Unscientific Postscript on Schleiermacher," in idem, *The Theology of Schleiermacher,* ed. Dietrich Ritschl, trans. Geoffrey W. Bromiley (Grand Rapids, Mich.: Eerdmans, 1982), 264.

27. Ibid., 270–71.

28. Karl Barth, "The Christian Faith," in idem, *The Theology of Schleiermacher,* 210.

29. Barth, *Die kirchliche Dogmatik,* 3/1 (Zurich: Evangelischer Verlag, 1945), ix.

30. Harold Nebelsick, "Karl Barth's Understanding of Science," in *Theology beyond Christendom: Essays on the Centenary of the Birth of Karl Barth, May 10, 1886,* ed. John Thompson (Allison Park, Pa.: Pickwick Publications, 1986), 201.

31. Ibid., 201. See also idem, *Theology and Science in Mutual Modification* (New York: Oxford University Press, 1981), 159ff.

32. *The Phenomenon of Man* was published in New York by Harper and Row in 1959, with a revised edition coming out in 1965. *The Divine Milieu* came out from the same publisher in 1960. The original French versions of these and other works have likewise been translated into many other languages.

33. Of the many books written about Teilhard, a useful entrée remains N. M. Wildiers, *An Introduction to Teilhard de Chardin,* trans. Hubert Hoskins (New York: Harper and Row, 1968).

34. See Karl Rahner, *Science and Christian Faith,* vol. 21 of *Theological Investigations,* trans. Hugh M. Riley (New York: Crossroad, 1988), as well as such essays as "Science as a 'Confession'?" in vol. 3 of the series (Baltimore: Helicon, 1967), 385–400, and "Christology within an Evolutionary View of the World" in vol. 5 (Baltimore: Helicon, 1966), 157–92.

35. Karl Rahner, "The Experience of God Today," in *Theological Investigations,* vol. 11, trans. David Bourke (New York: Seabury, 1974), 155–56.

36. Rahner, "Science as a 'Confession'?" 389.

37. Ibid., 391.

38. Karl Rahner, *Foundations of Christian Faith: An Introduction to the Idea of Christianity,* trans. William V. Dych (New York: Crossroad, 1984), 88–89.

2. Cosmology and the Doctrine of Creation

1. Pope Pius XII, "Modern Science and the Existence of God," *Catholic Mind* 50 (March 1952):184. The original Italian version of the address is to be found in *Acta Apostolicae Sedis* 44 (1952):31–43.

2. Ibid., 191.

3. Pope John Paul II, "The Path of Scientific Discovery," *Origins* 11.18 (15 October 1981):279.

4. Quentin Smith, "Atheism, Theism, and Big Bang Cosmology," in William Lane Craig and Quentin Smith, *Theism, Atheism, and Big Bang Cosmology* (Oxford: Clarendon Press, 1993, 1995), 199.

5. The following are helpful resources for the non-specialist: Timothy Ferris, *The Whole Shebang: A State-of-the-Universe(s) Report* (New York: Simon & Schuster, 1997); George Ellis, *Before the Beginning: Cosmology Explained* (London: Boyars/Bowerdean, 1993); and Steven Weinberg, *The First Three Minutes* (New York: Basic Books, 1977).

6. William R. Stoeger, S.J., "Contemporary Cosmology and Its Implications for the Science-Religion Dialogue," in *Physics, Philosophy, and Theology: A Common Quest for Understanding,* ed. Robert John Russell et al., 3rd ed. (Vatican City State: Vatican Observatory Foundation, 1997), 222.

7. Willem Drees, "A Case Against Temporal Critical Realism? Consequences of Quantum Cosmology for Theology," in *Quantum Cosmology and the Laws of Nature: Scientific Perspectives on Divine Action,* ed. Robert John Russell et al., 2nd ed. (Vatican City State: Vatican Observatory Foundation; Berkeley, Calif.: Center for Theology and the Natural Sciences, 1996), 333.

8. John Polkinghorne, "More to the World Than Meets the Eye," in *Religion and the Natural Sciences: The Range of Engagement,* ed. James E. Huchingson (Fort Worth: Harcourt Brace, 1993), 238.

9. Ernan McMullin, "Natural Science and Belief in a Creator," in *Physics, Philosophy, and Theology,* 70.

10. Fred Hoyle, *The Nature of the Universe* (New York: Mentor, 1950), 125. Similarly, in his astronomy textbook Hoyle wrote that many people are happy to accept the position that the universe had an absolute beginning in time since they are then able to introduce a "something" outside physics at that point. "By a semantic manoeuvre, the word 'something' is then replaced by 'god', except that the first letter becomes a capital, God, in order to warn us that we must not carry the enquiry any further" (*Astronomy and Cosmology: A Modern Course* [San Francisco: W. H. Freeman, 1975], 685).

11. Stephen Hawking, *A Brief History of Time: From the Big Bang to Black Holes* (New York: Bantam Books, 1988), 136. Some have conjectured that Hawking, like Hoyle, has developed his position at least in part out of non-theistic leanings. Lutheran theologian Ted Peters writes: "Might we view Hawking as belonging to the subculture of natural scientists who, on the one hand, drive as big a wedge as possible between rational science and allegedly irrational religion, while, on the other hand, invoking scientific discoveries to buttress their belief that belief in God is out of date?" (Ted Peters, "The Trinity in and beyond Time," in *Quantum Cosmology and the Laws of Nature,* 278). Peters goes on to suggest that the God that Hawking seems to be rejecting is only the God of deism, a being responsible only for the beginning of the universe, after which the deity retires from the scene.

12. For a brief overview of these theories, see Lawrence Osborn, "Theology and the New Physics," chapter 3 of *God, Humanity, and the Cosmos,* ed. Christopher Southgate et al. (Harrisburg, Pa.: Trinity Press International, 1999), 126–27.

13. Hawking, *A Brief History of Time,* 139.

14. Arthur Peacocke, *Creation and the World of Science: The Bampton Lectures, 1978* (Oxford: Clarendon Press, 1979), 46.

15. Stoeger, "Contemporary Cosmology," 240.

16. Richard J. Clifford, S.J., and Roland E. Murphy, O.Carm., "Genesis," in *The New Jerome Biblical Commentary,* ed. Raymond E. Brown et al. (Englewood Cliffs, N.J.: Prentice Hall, 1990), 10.

17. *Genesis,* Introduction, translation, and notes by E. A. Speiser, The Anchor Bible (Garden City, N.Y.: Doubleday, 1964), 3.

18. Further details about this distinction may be found in Jürgen Moltmann, *God in Creation: A New Theology of Creation and the Spirit of God,* trans. Margaret Kohl (San Francisco: Harper and Row, 1985), 73.

19. Tatian, *Oratio ad graecos* 5.

20. Theophilus of Antioch, *Ad Autolycum* 2, 4 (trans. W. A. Jurgens, *The Faith of the Early Fathers,* vol. 1 [Collegeville, Minn.: Liturgical Press, 1970], 75).

21. Irenaeus, *Adversus haereses* 2, 10, 4 (trans. Jurgens, 87).

22. Augustine, *Confessions* 11, 14 (trans. R. S. Pine-Coffin [Harmondsworth and New York: Penguin, 1961], 263).

23. Thomas Aquinas, *Summa theologiae* I, q. 46, a. 2 (trans. English Dominicans [New York: Benziger, 1947], 1:243).

24. Ibid., I, q. 46, a. 2, ad 2.

25. The two phrases in quotation marks are taken from Robert John Russell, "Finite Creation without a Beginning: The Doctrine of Creation in Relation to Big Bang and Quantum Cosmologies," in *Quantum Cosmology and the Laws of Nature* (note 7), 294. In somewhat different terminology, Antony Flew has made the same basic point: "If the world was eternal and had no beginning, then there would be no room for creation, in this [popular] sense. In the second, the theological sense, questions about creation are questions about an absolute onto-logical dependence to which particular scientific discoveries are simply irrelevant. This distinction is important; but difficult, because almost everyone—including St. Thomas—who has believed in creation in the second sense has also believed that the world had a beginning, and that it was in the first sense, also, created" (A. Flew and A. MacIntyre, *New Essays in Philosophical Theology* [New York: Macmillan, 1955], 174).

26. Peacocke, *Creation and the World of Science*, 78.

27. Keith Ward, "God as a Principle of Cosmological Explanation," in *Quantum Cosmology and the Laws of Nature* (note 7), 248–49.

28. Moltmann, *God in Creation*, 78.

29. Ted Peters, "On Creating the Cosmos," in *Physics, Philosophy, and Theology*, 288.

30. For further details, see Hugh Ross, Ph.D., "Design Evidences in the Cos-mos." Updated 1998. Viewed 24 November 2000. <http://www.reasons.org/resources/apologetics/designevidenceupdate1998.html>.

31. George Greenstein, *The Symbiotic Universe: Life and Mind in the Cosmos* (New York: William Morrow, 1988), 26–27.

32. P. C. W. Davies, "The Intelligiblity of Nature," in *Quantum Cosmology and the Laws of Nature* (note 7), 160–61.

33. McMullin, "Natural Science and Belief in a Creator," 71.

34. Nick Bostrum, Ph.D., "The Anthropic Principle." Updated 15 June 2000. Viewed 24 November 2000. <http://www.anthropic-principle.com>.

35. Ian Barbour, "Creation and Cosmology," in *Cosmos and Creation*, 134.

36. Stoeger, "Contemporary Cosmology," 221.

37. Joseph M. Zycinski, "Metaphysics and Epistemology in Stephen Hawk-ing's Theory of the Creation of the Universe," *Zygon* 31 (1996):271.

38. J. Wentzel van Huyssteen, *Duet or Duel: Theology and Science in a Post-modern World* (Harrisburg, Pa.: Trinity Press International, 1998), 68. Consider, too, these words of William Stoeger: "It seems highly unlikely that cosmology, or any physical science, will ever be able to unveil a point of *absolute* begin-ning—before which *nothing* existed, before which time of any sort was not—which would require the direct influence of God. That does not mean that such an event did not occur. It does mean that cosmology is *not* able to discover it and reveal it as the 'Ur-event,' the event needing other than secondary causes for its immediate explanation" ("Contemporary Cosmology and Its Implications for the Science-Religion Dialogue," 240).

39. Peters, "Cosmos as Creation," 107.

40. Quentin Smith, *The Felt Meanings of the World: A Metaphysics of Feeling* (West Lafayette, Ind.: Purdue University Press, 1986), 300–301.

41. Zycinski, "Metaphysics and Epistemology," 282.

42. Quentin Smith, "A Criticism of A Posteriori and A Priori Arguments for a Cause of the Big Bang Singularity," in *Theism, Atheism and Big Bang Cosmology,* 182–83.

43. William Lane Craig, "A Criticism of the Cosmological Argument for God's Non-existence," ibid., 275.

44. Ward, "God as a Principle of Cosmological Explanation," 258.

45. Michael Heller, "On Theological Interpretations of Physical Creation Theories," in *Quantum Cosmology and the Laws of Nature* (note 7), 99.

46. Ellis, "The Theology of the Anthropic Principle," 381.

47. Pierre Teilhard de Chardin, "The Mass on the World," in idem, *Hymn of the Universe,* trans. Simon Bartholomew (New York and Evanston: Harper and Row, 1965), 21–22.

48. Stoeger, "Contemporary Cosmology," 240.

3. Evolution and the Doctrine of Divine Providence

1. Richard Owen, *On the Archetypes and Homologies of the Vertebrate Skeleton* (1848), quoted by John Durant, "A Critical-Historical Perspective on the Argument about Evolution and Creation," in *An Evolving Dialogue: Scientific, Historical, Philosophical and Theological Perspectives on Evolution* (Washington, D.C.: American Association for the Advancement of Science, 1998), 271.

2. David J. Depew and Bruce H. Weber, *Darwinism Evolving: Systems Dynamics and the Genealogy of Natural Selection* (Cambridge, Mass., and London: MIT Press, A Bradford Book, 1995), 111.

3. For Darwin's own account of his religious position late in life, see the autobiography that he originally composed for his grandchildren: Charles Darwin, Thomas Henry Huxley, *Autobiographies,* ed. Gavin de Beer (London and New York: Oxford University Press, 1974), esp. 50–54.

4. John Hedley Brooke, *Science and Religion: Some Historical Perspectives* (Cambridge: Cambridge University Press, 1991), 41.

5. George Gaylord Simpson, *This View of Life* (New York: Harcourt, Brace and World, 1964), quoted by Depew and Weber, 318.

6. Richard Dawkins, *River Out of Eden* (New York: HarperCollins, 1995), 133.

7. See, e.g., Daniel Dennett, *Darwin's Dangerous Idea* (New York: Simon and Schuster, 1995) and William Provine, "Evolution and the Foundation of Ethics," in *Science, Technology, and Social Progress,* ed. Steven L. Goldman (Bethlehem, Pa.: Lehigh University Press, 1989).

8. Perhaps the best-known example of Lamarck's argument for the inheritance of an acquired characteristic was that of a giraffe acquiring a longer and longer neck as a result of stretching for food higher and higher up on trees and then producing offspring whose necks would likewise tend to be longer than average. A claim of this sort, at least in this simplistic form, has not been verified. A Darwinian approach to the same phenomenon would be quite different: Among a population of giraffes, some would happen to have longer necks than others and, in a particular tree-rich environment, would thereby be able to reach more

leaves, be better-fed and healthier, and so tend to produce more young and rear them to reproductive age.

9. Charles Darwin, *Autobiography,* 71.

10. Charles Darwin, *On the Origin of Species by Means of Natural Selection,* ch. 3, Great Books of the Western World, vol. 49 (Chicago and London: Encyclopedia Britannica, Inc., 1952), 32.

11. On this last-named factor, see in particular Stuart Kauffman, *The Origins of Order: Self-Organization and Selection in Evolution* (New York: Oxford University Press, 1993). For a history of developments in evolutionary theory over the past two centuries, see Depew and Weber, *Darwinism Evolving* (note 2 above).

12. Arthur Caplan, "The Facts Back Darwin," *Philadelphia Inquirer,* 23 February 2001. Viewed 24 February 2001. <http://cofaxing.philly.com/content/inquirer/2001/02/23/opinion/CAPLAN23.htm>.

13. Guy Gugliotta, "Comet Tied to a Mass Extinction," *Washington Post,* 23 February 2001, sec. A, p. 3.

14. Depew and Weber, *Darwinism Evolving,* 422.

15. Francisco Ayala, "Chance and Necessity: Adaptation and Novelty in Evolution," in *An Evolving Dialogue* (note 1), 250.

16. Kenneth R. Miller, *Finding Darwin's God: A Scientist's Search for Common Ground Between God and Evolution* (New York: HarperCollins, Cliff Street Books, 1999).

17. Ibid., 173.

18. Michael J. Behe, *Darwin's Black Box* (New York: The Free Press, 1996).

19. William Paley, *Natural Theology,* chapter 3, anthologized in *Science and Religion in the Nineteenth Century,* ed. Tess Cosslett (Cambridge and New York: Cambridge University Press, 1984), 41.

20. Ibid., 44–45.

21. This is discussed by Miller, *Finding Darwin's God,* 150–51, with reference to the study of Enrique Meléndez-Hevia et al., "The Puzzle of the Krebs Citric Acid Cycle: Assembling the Pieces of Chemically Feasible Reactions, and Opportunism in the Design of Metabolic Pathways during Evolution," *Journal of Molecular Evolution* 43 (1996):293–303.

22. Behe, *Darwin's Black Box,* 228.

23. Miller, *Finding Darwin's God,* 162.

24. Ibid.

25. William A. Dembski and Michael J. Behe, *Intelligent Design: The Bridge between Science and Theology* (Downers Grove, Ill.: InterVarsity Press, 1999) and William A. Dembski, *The Design Inference* (Cambridge and New York: Cambridge University Press, 1998).

26. William A. Dembski, "Teaching Intelligent Design: What Happened When? A Response to Eugenie Scott." Metaviews, ID 2675. 22 February 2001. Viewed 6 March 2001. <http://www.metanexus.net>.

27. Richard Dawkins, interviewed on *Faith and Reason,* written by Margaret Wertheim, 55 min., New River Media, 1998, videocassette.

28. Pope John Paul II, "Message to the Pontifical Academy of Sciences

on Evolution," *Origins: Catholic News Service Documentary Service* 26.22 (24 November 1996):352.

29. John F. Haught, *God After Darwin: A Theology of Evolution* (Boulder, Colo.: Westview Press, 2000).

30. John F. Haught, "Response to Behe Review of *God After Darwin.*" Metaviews, ID 3092. 10 December 1999. Viewed 6 March 2001. <http://www.metanexus.net>.

31. John Henry Newman, letter to W. R. Brownlow (afterwards Bishop of Clifton), 13 April 1870, quoted in Wilfrid Ward, *The Life of John Henry Newman, Based on His Private Journals and Correspondence*, 2 vols. (London: Longmans, Green, 1912), 2:269.

32. Haught, *God After Darwin*, 94.

33. Depew and Weber, *Darwinism Evolving*, 395.

34. Paul Davies, "Teleology without Teleology: Purpose through Emergent Complexity," in *Evolutionary and Molecular Biology: Scientific Perspectives on Divine Action*, ed. Robert John Russell et al. (Vatican City State: Vatican Observatory Publications; Berkeley, Calif.: Center for Theology and the Natural Sciences, 1998), 160; Haught, *God After Darwin*, 131.

35. Karl Schmitz-Moormann, *Theology of Creation in an Evolutionary World* (Cleveland: Pilgrim Press, 1997), 48.

36. John Haught, "Does Evolution Rule Out God's Existence?" in *An Evolving Dialogue* (note 1), 350. This piece is a revision of the second chapter of Haught's *Science and Religion: From Conflict to Conversation* (New York: Paulist Press, 1996).

37. Haught, *God After Darwin*, 53.

38. Depew and Weber, *Darwinism Evolving*, 187 and 510, n. 5.

39. Haught, *God After Darwin*, 177.

40. Charles Birch, "Neo-Darwinism, Self-organization, and Divine Action," in *Evolutionary and Molecular Biology* (note 34), 247.

41. Ian Barbour, "Five Models of God and Evolution," ibid., 437–38.

42. Schmitz-Moormann, *Theology of Creation in an Evolutionary World*, 123.

43. See Russell Stannard, *The God Experiment* (Mahwah, N.J.: Paulist Press, 2000), 143.

44. Stephen Jay Gould, "The Evolution of Life on Earth," in *An Evolving Dialogue* (note 1), 162.

45. Haught, *God After Darwin*, 159.

46. Thomas Aquinas, *Summa theologiae* I, q. 22, a. 2, ad 1 (trans. Thomas Gilby, O.P. [London and New York: Blackfriars, 1967], 5:95).

47. Elizabeth A. Johnson, C.S.J., "Does God Play Dice? Divine Providence and Chance," *Theological Studies* 57 (1996):15.

48. Haught, "Does Evolution Rule Out God's Existence?" 350.

49. For further elucidation of this analogy, see Davies, "Teleology without Teleology" (note 34), 155. He there writes that "we may exploit the chess analogy and suggest that God, on the one hand, acts by selecting from the set of all possible laws of nature those laws that encourage or facilitate rich and interesting patterns of behavior, and these laws are inherently statistical. On the other hand,

the details of the actual evolution of the universe are left to the 'whims' of the players (including chance operating at the quantum or chaos level, the actions of human minds, etc.)."

4. Evolution and the Doctrine of the Human Soul

1. In this connection, John Haught writes that the scientific skeptic William Provine of Cornell University is unquestionably sincere in writing about the way his life is filled with meaning through his happy marriage, wonderful children, fulfilling job, and loyal friends. This is not, however, what Haught means when he speaks of purpose or meaning in the universe, namely, "the belief, expressed paradigmatically in religions, that the cosmos is embraced by an incomprehensible divine mystery that promises an eternal significance and unimagined coherence to the sequence of happenings that make up evolution and our lives within it" (John Haught, *God After Darwin: A Theology of Evolution* [Boulder, Colo.: Westview Press, 2000], 122).

2. Pope John Paul II, "Message to the Pontifical Academy of Sciences on Evolution," *Origins: Catholic News Service Documentary Service* 26.22 (24 November 1996):352.

3. George Gaylord Simpson, *The Meaning of Evolution* (New Haven: Yale University Press, 1971), 258.

4. Aristotle, *Historia Animalium,* bk. 8 (588a18–31), trans. D'Arcy Wentworth Thompson, in *The Basic Works of Aristotle,* ed. Richard McKeon (New York: Random House, 1941), 634–35.

5. Jane Goodall, "Rain Dance," *Science & Spirit* (May–June 2001):23.

6. Pope John Paul II, "Message to the Pontifical Academy," 352.

7. Paul Badham, "Do Animals Have Immortal Souls?" in *Animals on the Agenda: Questions about Animals for Theology and Ethics,* ed. Andrew Linzey and Dorothy Yamamoto (London: SCM Press, 1998), 184.

8. Michael H. Barnes, review of *Whatever Happened to the Soul?* ed. Warren S. Brown et al., *Horizons: Journal of the College Theology Society* 26 (1999):386.

9. Klaus Kremer, "Zur Einführung: Die Problemlage und die Aufgabe," in *Seele: Ihre Wirklichkeit, ihr Verhältnis zum Leib und zur menschlichen Person,* ed. idem (Leiden and Cologne: Brill, 1984), 8.

10. Daniel Dennett, *Consciousness Explained* (New York: Little, Brown, 1991), 33.

11. John Polkinghorne, "Science and Theology in the Twenty-First Century," *Zygon* 35 (2000):948.

12. Dennett, *Consciousness Explained,* 33.

13. Malcolm Jeeves, "Brain, Mind, and Behavior," in *Whatever Happened to the Soul?* ed. Warren S. Brown et al. (Minneapolis: Fortress, 1998), 89.

14. Nancey Murphy, "Human Nature: Historical, Scientific, and Religious Issues," ibid., 18–19.

15. C. A. van Peursen, *Body, Soul, Spirit: A Survey of the Body-Mind Problem,* trans. Hubert H. Hoskins (London: Oxford University Press, 1966), 172.

16. As in their co-authored book *The Self and Its Brain: An Argument for Interactionism* (New York: Springer International, 1977).

17. Joachim Jeremias, *Theologisches Wörterbuch zum Neuen Testament*, s.v. "paradeisos," quoted by Joseph Ratzinger, *Eschatology: Death and Eternal Life*, trans. Michael Waldstein (Washington, D.C.: The Catholic University of America Press, 1988), 125.

18. Ratzinger, *Eschatology*, 109.

19. Ibid., 259.

20. M. James C. Crabbe, "Introduction" to *From Soul to Self*, ed. idem (London and New York: Routledge, 1999), 3.

21. Richard Sorabji, "Soul and Self in Ancient Philosophy," in *From Soul to Self* (note 20), 22.

22. Maurice Leenhardt, *Do Kamo: La personne et le mythe dans le monde mélanésien* (Paris, 1947), quoted by van Peursen (note 15), 85. English translation: *Do Kamo: Person and Myth in the Melanesian World*, trans. Basia Miller Gulati (Chicago: University of Chicago Press, 1979).

23. van Peursen, *Body, Soul, Spirit*, 85.

24. *Odyssey* 24:1–2, 11–22 (trans. Richard Lattimore [New York: Harper-Collins, Perennial Books, 1991], 345).

25. Thus, Gisbert Greshake writes that the ancient Greek notions of the soul and the world of the dead are "not very different from the Old Testament understandings of *nephesh* and Sheol" (Gisbert Greshake and Jacob Kremer, *Resurrectio Mortuorum: Zum theologischen Verständis der leiblichen Auferstehung* [Darmstadt: Wissenschaftliche Buchgesellschaft, 1986), 169.

26. *Phaedo* 66b–67a (trans. Hugh Tredennick in *The Collected Dialogues of Plato*, ed. Edith Hamilton and Huntington Cairns [New York: Random House, Pantheon Books, 1961], 49).

27. Consider, e.g., his statement in book eleven of the *Laws* that we should honor our parents and other ancestors, since their person "is, in truth, an image of God more marvelous than any lifeless statue" (931d).

28. Ratzinger, *Eschatology*, 149.

29. John Calvin, *Institutes of the Christian Religion* (1559 ed.) 3.25.5 (trans. Ford Lewis Battles in *Calvin's Institutes: A New Compend*, ed. Hugh T. Kerr [Louisville: Westminster/John Knox Press, 1989], 124).

30. Descartes, *Meditation II*, in *The Philosophical Writings of Descartes*, vol. 2, trans. J. Cottingham (Cambridge: Cambridge University Press, 1984), 18.

31. Descartes, Letter to the Marquess of Newcastle, 1646, in idem, *Philosophical Letters*, trans. and ed. Anthony Kenny (Oxford: Clarendon Press, 1970), 207.

32. *Catechism of the Catholic Church*, no. 366 (New York: Paulist Press, 1994), 93. The footnote to this passage refers to Pope Pius XII's encyclical *Humani Generis*, to Pope Paul VI's *Credo of the People of God*, and to the decrees of the Fifth Lateran Council (1513).

33. *The New Dictionary of Theology*, ed. Joseph A. Komonchak et al. (Wilmington, Del.: Michael Glazier, 1987).

34. Ratzinger, *Eschatology*, 105.

35. Martin Luther, *Tischreden*, quoted by Ratzinger, *Eschatology*, 119.

36. Joan Acker, "Creationism and the Catechism: Observations of a Sister Scientist," *America* 183, no. 20 (16 December 2000):9.

37. Ratzinger, *Eschatology,* 259.

38. See, e.g., Oscar Cullmann, *Immortality of the Soul or Resurrection of the Dead? The Witness of the New Testament* (London: Epworth, 1958). This was the annual Ingersoll Lecture, delivered at Harvard University on 26 April 1955.

39. Zachary Hayes, *Visions of a Future: A Study of Christian Eschatology* (Collegeville, Minn.: Liturgical Press, 1990), 109.

40. Bernard of Clairvaux, *On Loving God* XI.30, in *Bernard of Clairvaux: Selected Works,* trans. G. R. Evans (New York: Paulist, 1987), 197.

41. Wolfgang Kluxen, "Seele und Unsterblichkeit bei Thomas von Aquin," in Kremer, ed., *Seele* (note 9), 83.

42. A. R. van de Walle writes: "No one who has a personal devotion for a particular saint thinks for a moment that this saint is not completely happy but is still yearning for the resurrection of the body. Moreover, in popular piety saints normally appear as *human beings*. People regularly and easily consider them to be glorified human beings in heaven. One never thinks of them as souls" (*Bis zum Anbruch der Morgenröte: Grundriss einer christlichen Eschatologie,* quoted by Greshake, *Resurrectio Mortuorum* [note 25], 268).

43. Karl Rahner, "The Interpretation of the Dogma of the Assumption," in idem, *Theological Investigations,* vol. 1, trans. Cornelius Ernst, O.P. (Baltimore: Helicon, 1961), 225.

44. See, e.g., Donald Senior, O.P., "The Death of Jesus and the Resurrection of the Holy Ones (Mt 27:51–53)," *The Catholic Biblical Quarterly* 38 (1976):314.

45. John Meier, *The Vision of Matthew: Christ, Church, and Morality in the First Gospel* (New York: Paulist Press, 1979), 204–5.

46. St. Francis de Sales, "Sur les vertus de saint Joseph," in *Oeuvres de saint François de Sales,* vol. 6, *Les vrays entretiens spirituels* (Annecy: J. Niérat, 1895), 369.

47. Rahner, "Interpretation of the Dogma," 226.

48. Saying that not everyone who dies necessarily enters into the "community of the redeemed" raises not only the question of the possibility of eternal damnation for persons who may have utterly closed themselves to God's offer of communion but also the issue of a purificatory state (Purgatory) and whether it makes sense to speak of this in terms of temporal duration rather than of "intensive purgation" at the time of death. It would not be germane to enter into these questions here. For the reflections of one prominent theologian on the question of a purificatory state, see Karl Rahner, "Purgatory," in idem, *Theological Investigations,* vol. 19, trans. Edward Quinn (New York: Crossroad, 1983), 181-93.

49. Joseph Ratzinger, "Resurrection: B. Theological," in *Sacramentum Mundi: An Encyclopedia of Theology* (New York: Herder and Herder, 1970), 5:340.

50. Ratzinger, *Eschatology,* 259.

51. Ratzinger, "Zwischen Tod und Auferstehung," *Internationale katholische Zeitschrift: Communio* 9 (1980):218, quoted by Greshake, *Resurrectio Mortuorum,* 267.

52. For examples drawn from the acts of early martyrs like Pionios and Fructuosus (both third century), see Greshake, *Resurrectio Mortuorum,* 182–83.

53. Karl Rahner, "The Intermediate State," in idem, *Theological Investigations,* vol. 17, trans. Margaret Kohl (New York: Crossroad, 1981), 121.

54. Ibid., 124.

55. Annie Dillard, *Pilgrim at Tinker Creek: A Mystical Excursion into the Natural World* (New York: Harper and Row, 1974), 124.

56. Elizabeth A. Johnson, "Presidential Address: Turn to the Heavens and the Earth: Retrieval of the Cosmos in Theology," The Catholic Theological Society of America, *Proceedings of the Fifty-first Annual Convention* 51 (1996):13.

57. Ibid., 14.

58. Richard Swinburne, *The Evolution of Soul* (Oxford: Clarendon Press, 1986), 183.

59. John Wesley, "The General Deliverance," in idem, *Sermons on Several Occasions,* vol. 2 (London: Wesleyan Conference Office, 1874), 281–86, anthologized in *Animals and Christianity: A Book of Readings,* ed. Andrew Linzey and Tom Regan (New York: Crossroad, 1988), 102–3.

60. Petroc Willey and Eldred Willey, "Will Animals Be Redeemed?" in Andrew Linzey and Dorothy Yamamoto, eds., *Animals on the Agenda: Questions about Animals for Theology and Ethics* (London: SCM Press, 1998), 194.

61. Kallistos Ware, "The Soul in Greek Christianity," in Crabbe, ed., *From Soul to Self* (note 20), 64.

62. Thomas E. Hosinski, "How Does God's Providential Care Extend to Animals?" in Linzey and Yamamoto, eds., *Animals on the Agenda* (note 60), 143.

63. Dante, *Paradiso* 3:70–72, 79–85 (trans. Charles S. Singleton [Princeton, N.J.: Princeton University Press, 1975], 31–33).

64. Andrew Linzey, Introduction to part three of *Animals on the Agenda* (note 60), 119.

5. Cosmology and the Doctrine of Eschatology

1. Bede, *A History of the English Church and People,* trans. Leo Sherley-Price (Harmondsworth and Baltimore: Penguin, 1955), 125.

2. Robert John Russell offers personal reflections about his observation of this particular star in his paper "God and Contemporary Cosmology: Continuing the Creative Interaction," in *God, Science, and Humility: Ten Scientists Consider Humility Theology,* ed. Robert L. Herrmann (Philadelphia and London: Templeton Foundation Press, 2000), 26–51, esp. 42–44.

3. Arnold Benz, *The Future of the Universe: Chance, Chaos, God?* (New York and London: Continuum, 2000), 141. The rest of my paragraph is drawn largely from material in this part of Benz's book.

4. Timothy Ferris, *The Whole Shebang: A State of the Universe(s) Report* (New York: Simon & Schuster, 1997), 78.

5. Kathy Sawyer, "Supernova Observations Bolster 'Dark Energy' Theory," *Washington Post,* 3 April 2001, sec. A, p. 3.

6. Benz, *The Future of the Universe,* 147. For a more detailed discussion of this process, see Fred C. Adams and Gregory Laughlin, "A Dying Universe: The

Long-Term Fate and Evolution of Astrophysical Objects," *Review of Modern Physics* 69 (1997):337–72.

7. Steven Weinberg, *The First Three Minutes* (New York: Basic Books, 1977), 149.

8. Peter Atkins, " 'There Is No God': An Interview with Peter Atkins," *The World and I* 16, no. 5 (May 2001):152.

9. Gerhard Sauter, "Our Reasons for Hope," in *The End of the World and the Ends of God: Science and Theology on Eschatology,* ed. John Polkinghorne and Michael Welker (Harrisburg, Pa.: Trinity Press International, 2000), 219.

10. Russell, "God and Contemporary Cosmology," 44.

11. John Macquarrie, *Principles of Christian Theology,* 2nd ed. (New York: Charles Scribner's Sons, 1977), 356.

12. John Polkinghorne, "Creation and the Structure of the Physical World," *Theology Today* 44 (April 1987–January 1988):66.

13. Rosemary Radford Ruether, *Sexism and God-Talk: Towards a Feminist Theology* (Boston and London: Beacon Press, 1983), 257.

14. Jürgen Moltmann, *The Coming of God: Christian Eschatology,* trans. Margaret Kohl (Minneapolis: Fortress, 1996), 276–77.

15. Ibid., 260.

16. John Polkinghorne, *The Faith of a Physicist: Reflections of a Bottom-Up Thinker* (Princeton, N.J.: Princeton University Press, 1994), 167.

17. John Polkinghorne, "Eschatology: Some Questions and Some Insights from Science," in *The End of the World and the Ends of God* (note 9), 39.

18. Zachary Hayes, *What Are They Saying About the End of the World?* (New York: Paulist Press, 1983), 51.

19. Ted Peters, *God as Trinity* (Louisville: Westminster/John Knox Press, 1994), 176. The British theologians Richard Bauckham and Trevor Hart take a similar position in writing that eschatology has to do "not with the best that can be hoped for from and in this world, but with a new world which will be brought into being only when God wills and acts to do so. The conditions for this future . . . will be created by God himself out of the abyss of non-being on the cusp of which our world and its inhabitants exist precariously from moment to moment. . . . " ("The Shape of Time," in *The Future as God's Gift: Explorations in Christian Eschatology,* ed. David Fergusson and Marcel Sarot [Edinburgh: T&T Clark, 2000], 70).

20. Raymond E. Brown, *An Introduction to the New Testament* (New York: Doubleday, 1997), 776.

21. Ibid., 775.

22. Edward Schillebeeckx, *Church: The Human Story of God,* trans. John Bowden (New York: Crossroad, 1990), 133.

23. Gale Z. Heide, "What Is New About the New Heaven and the New Earth? A Theology of Creation from Revelation 21 and 2 Peter 3," *Journal of the Evangelical Theological Society* 40 (1997):55.

24. Karl Rahner, "The Hermeneutics of Eschatological Assertions," in idem, *Theological Investigations,* vol. 4, trans. Kevin Smyth (Baltimore: Helicon, 1966), 336, note 12.

25. Commenting on this propensity among some theologians, John Jefferson Davis writes: "Notable examples from the history of science...show that Christian theologians went beyond the bounds of their proper competence when they attempted to substitute biblical exegesis for empirical research or to impose traditional interpretations of biblical texts regarding natural matters on the natural scientists" ("Cosmic Endgame: Theological Reflections on Recent Scientific Speculations on the Ultimate Fate of the Universe," *Science and Christian Belief* 11 [1999]:26).

26. Kathryn Tanner, "Eschatology without a Future?" in *The End of the World* (note 9), 223.

27. Ibid., 224.

28. Rudolf Bultmann, "The New Testament and Mythology," in idem, *Kerygma and Myth,* ed. Hans Werner Bartsch (New York: Harper, Torchbooks, 1961), 5.

29. Brown, *Introduction,* 810.

30. Polkinghorne, *The Faith of a Physicist,* 163. Karl Rahner once made a similar point when he wrote: "History and its consummated finality are distinguished from one another by that which is experienced in the personal history of the individual as death" ("The Theological Problems Entailed in the Idea of the 'New Earth,'" in idem, *Theological Investigations,* vol. 10, trans. David Bourke [New York: Herder and Herder, 1973], 269).

31. Moltmann, *The Coming of God,* 260.

32. Willem B. Drees, *Beyond the Big Bang: Quantum Cosmologies and God* (LaSalle, Ill.: Open Court, 1990), 117–18 and 150–54.

33. Sauter, "Our Reasons for Hope," 221.

34. Wilfrid Harrington, O.P., *Revelation,* Sacra Pagina series, vol. 16 (Collegeville, Minn.: Liturgical Press, 1993), 210.

35. Lynn White Jr., "The Historical Roots of Our Ecologic Crisis," *Science* 155 (10 March 1967):1203–7.

36. Ibid., 1205.

37. Ibid.

38. Elizabeth A. Johnson, *Women, Earth, and Creator Spirit* (New York: Paulist Press, 1993), 30.

39. H. Paul Santmire, *The Travail of Nature: The Ambiguous Ecological Promise of Christian Theology* (Philadelphia: Fortress Press, 1985), 119.

40. Patricia Mische, "Toward a Global Spirituality," *The Whole Earth Papers,* no. 16 (New York: Global Education Associates, 1982), 10.

41. Roger Burggraeve, "Responsibility for a 'New Heaven and a New Earth,'" in *No Heaven without Earth* (*Concilium* 1991/4), ed. Johann Baptist Metz and Edward Schillebeeckx (London: SCM Press; Philadelphia: Trinity Press International, 1991), 109.

42. Pope John Paul II, "Peace with All Creation" (Message on the World Day of Peace, 1 January 1990), *Origins: Catholic News Service Documentary Service* 19.28 (14 December 1989):465.

6. The Causal Continuum of Space-Time Events and Divine Action

1. Wolfhart Pannenberg, "Confessions of a Trinitarian Evolutionist: Thomas Jay Oord's Interview with Wolfhart Pannenberg — Part One." Metaviews, ID 3136. 19 May 2001. Viewed on same date. <http://www.metanexus.net>.

2. Langdon Gilkey, "Cosmology, Ontology, and Biblical Language," *Journal of Religion* 41 (1961):199.

3. Ibid., 195.

4. Dennis Bielfeldt, "Can Western Monotheism Avoid Substance Dualism?" *Zygon* 36 (2001):155.

5. Philip Clayton, "Neuroscience, the Person, and God: An Emergentist Account," in *Neuroscience and the Person: Scientific Perspectives on Divine Action,* ed. Robert John Russell et al. (Vatican City State: Vatican Observatory Publications; Berkeley, Calif.: Center for Theology and the Natural Sciences, 1999), 209.

6. Nicholas T. Saunders, "Does God Cheat at Dice? Divine Action and Quantum Possibilities." *Zygon* 35 (2000):518.

7. William G. Pollard, *Chance and Providence: God's Action in a World Governed by Scientific Law* (London: Faber and Faber, 1958), 12.

8. It may be found, e.g., in *Kerygma and Myth,* ed. Hans Werner Bartsch (New York: Harper, Torchbooks, 1961), 1–44.

9. Paul D. Murray, "Truth and Reason in Science and Theology," chapter 2 of *God, Humanity, and the Cosmos,* ed. Christopher Southgate et al. (Harrisburg, Pa.: Trinity Press International, 1999), 55.

10. See Donald T. Campbell, "'Downward Causation' in Hierarchically Organized Systems," in *Studies in the Philosophy of Biology: Reduction and Related Problems,* ed. Francisco J. Ayala and Theodosius Dobzhansky (London: Macmillan, 1974), 179–86.

11. Arthur Peacocke, *Theology for a Scientific Age: Being and Becoming — Natural, Divine, and Human* (Minneapolis: Fortress Press, 1993), 53–54.

12. Peacocke, "The Sound of Sheer Silence: How Does God Communicate with Humanity?" in *Neuroscience and the Person* (note 5), 221.

13. Ibid., 236.

14. Ibid., 235.

15. Philip Clayton, *God and Contemporary Science* (Grand Rapids, Mich.: Eerdmans, 1997), 227.

16. Philip Clayton, "Neuroscience, the Person, and God: An Emergentist Account," in *Neuroscience and the Person* (note 5), 205.

17. A useful introduction to quantum theory is Nick Herbert's *Quantum Reality: Beyond the New Physics* (New York: Doubleday, Anchor Books, 1985).

18. See their co-authored *On the Moral Nature of the Universe: Theology, Cosmology, and Ethics* (Minneapolis: Fortress Press, 1996).

19. G. F. R. Ellis, "The Theology of the Anthropic Principle," in *Quantum Cosmology and the Laws of Nature: Scientific Perspectives on Divine Action,* ed. Robert John Russell et al., 2nd ed. (Vatican City State: Vatican Observatory Publications; Berkeley, Calif.: Center for Theology and the Natural Sciences, 1999),

391. Nicholas Saunders, while not at all advocating this position, explains it in the following way: Even though it seems that *we* cannot in principle know what an object described by quantum mechanics will do under every circumstance, "this indeterminism is not extended to God, who because of omniscience can see behind it and as such can control and manipulate it — achieving thereby specific aims from within the causal nexus in a way that is perfectly consonant with scientific regularity" ("Does God Cheat at Dice?" 521).

20. Nancey Murphy, "Divine Action in the Natural Order: Buridan's Ass and Schrödinger's Cat," in *Chaos and Complexity: Scientific Perspectives on Divine Action,* ed. Robert John Russell et al., 2nd ed. (Vatican City State: Vatican Observatory Publications; Berkeley, Calif.: The Center for Theology and the Natural Sciences, 2000), 349–50.

21. Ellis, "The Theology of the Anthropic Principle," 392–93.

22. Murphy, "Divine Action in the Natural Order," 343.

23. Ibid., 341. She later writes in the same essay: "Peacocke claims that God's action at the quantum level is forestalled by the fact that particular events are as unpredictable to God as to us. My proposal evades this difficulty since by hypothesis these events are not random; they are manifestations of divine will" (355).

24. Clayton, *God and Contemporary Science,* 218.

25. Saunders, "Does God Cheat at Dice?" 533.

26. Thomas Aquinas, *Summa Contra Gentiles* 3.70.5 (trans. Vernon J. Bourke in *On the Truth of the Catholic Faith.* Book Three: *Providence,* Part One [Garden City, N.Y.: Hanover House, 1956], 236).

27. On this point, Elizabeth A. Johnson comments: "God acts wholly through and in the finite agents that also act wholly in the event." The two "operate on completely different levels (itself an inadequate analogy), one being the cause of all causes and the other participating in this power" ("Does God Play Dice? Divine Providence and Chance," *Theological Studies* 57 [1996]:12).

28. Etienne Gilson, *The Christian Philosophy of St. Thomas Aquinas,* trans. L. K. Shook, C.S.B. (New York: Random House, 1956), 183.

29. Johnson, "Does God Play Dice?" 14–15.

30. Clayton, *God and Contemporary Science,* 224.

31. See, e.g., Grace Jantzen, *God's World, God's Body* (Philadelphia: Westminster Press, 1984) and Sallie McFague, *The Body of God: An Ecological Theology* (Minneapolis: Fortress Press, 1993).

32. Clayton, *God and Contemporary Science,* 264–65.

33. Ellis, "The Theology of the Anthropic Principle," 392.

34. Clayton, *God and Contemporary Science,* 194.

35. See, e.g., Nancey Murphy, "Divine Action in the Natural Order," 348–49. For a general introduction to the theory, see James Gleick, *Chaos: Making a New Science* (New York: Penguin, 1987).

36. As in Johnson, "Does God Play Dice?" 5–6.

37. Peter Smith, *Explaining Chaos* (Cambridge: Cambridge University Press, 1999), 67.

38. Jeffrey Kopeski, "God, Chaos, and the Quantum Dice," *Zygon* 35 (2000): 557.

39. Saunders, "Does God Cheat at Dice?" 523.

40. John Polkinghorne, *Science and Christian Belief: Reflections of a Bottom-up Thinker* (London: SPCK, 1994), 82. Farrer's works are *A Science of God?* (London: Geoffrey Bles, 1966) and *Faith and Speculation* (London: A. & C. Black, 1967). See also *Divine Action: Studies Inspired by the Philosophical Theology of Austin Farrer,* ed. Brian Hebblethwaite and Edward Henderson (Edinburgh: T&T Clark, 1991).

41. See Owen Thomas, "Recent Thought on Divine Agency," in *Divine Action* (note 40), 50.

42. Johnson, "Does God Play Dice?" 13.

43. This point is made by Christopher Southgate, "A Test Case — Divine Action," in *God, Humanity and the Cosmos* (note 9), 255.

44. Johnson, "Does God Play Dice?" 14–15.

45. Arthur Peacocke, "Guildhall Acceptance Speech" [on the occasion of receiving the 2001 Templeton Prize]. Metaviews, ID 3123. 10 May 2001. Viewed 17 May 2001. <http://www.metanexus.net>.

46. Thomas Aquinas, *Summa Theologiae* I, q. 105, a. 7 (trans. English Dominicans [New York: Benziger, 1947], 1:520).

47. John Meier, *A Marginal Jew: Rethinking the Historical Jesus,* vol. 2, *Mentor, Message, and Miracles* (New York: Doubleday, 1994), 512.

48. Alexis Carrel, *The Voyage to Lourdes,* trans. Virgilia Peterson (New York: Harper and Brothers, 1950); Louis Monden, *Signs and Wonders: A Study of the Miraculous Element in Religion* (New York and Paris: Desclée, 1966). Carrel's book contains a detailed account of how he, a thoroughgoing religious skeptic, was utterly confounded on seeing Marie Ferrand, dying of tubercular peritonitis, suddenly cured before his very eyes. The cure did not then and there convince him, but it was the beginning of the process of his eventual religious conversion.

49. Raymond E. Grizzle, "A Few Suggestions for the Proponents of Intelligent Design," *Perspectives on Science and Christian Faith* 47, no. 3 (September 1995):187.

50. Monden, *Signs and Wonders,* 234.

51. Diogenes Allen, "Faith and the Recognition of God's Activity," in *Divine Action* (note 40), 198.

52. St. John of the Cross, *The Ascent of Mount Carmel* 3.31.9 and 3.32.3 (trans. Kieran Kavanaugh, O.C.D., and Otilio Rodriguez, O.C.D., *The Collected Works of Saint John of the Cross,* rev. ed. [Washington, D.C.: I.C.S. Publications, 1991], 327–29).

53. Eliezer Shore, "The Milk of Miracle," *Parabola* (Winter 1997). Viewed 28 May 2001. <http://www.britannica.com/magazine?ebsco_id=325962>.

7. Essaying Coherence

1. Karl Rahner, "Science as a 'Confession'?" in idem, *Theological Investigations,* vol. 3, trans. Karl-H. and Boniface Kruger (Baltimore: Helicon, 1967), 391.

2. Karl Rahner, "Contemporary Youth and the Experience of God: Interview with Hubert Biallowons and Ferdinand Herget, Augsburg (1984)," trans.

Robert J. Braunreuther, S.J., in *Faith in a Wintry Season: Conversations and Interviews with Karl Rahner in the Last Years of His Life,* ed. Paul Imhof and Hubert Biallowons (New York: Crossroad, 1990), 108.

3. Gordon Kaufman, "On Thinking of God as Serendipitous Creativity," *Journal of the American Academy of Religion* 69 (2001):410.

4. Ibid., 412.

5. Ibid., 423. It is difficult to see just what it would mean to focus devotion and worship on the impersonal reality that Kaufman calls serendipitous creativity, though one cannot but applaud his ecological sensitivity and the forthright way in which he urges his readers to overcome "the destructive momentums we have already brought into the ecological order on planet Earth and into the historical order of human affairs" (Ibid., 417).

6. Ibid., 411, note 1.

7. Augustine, *Confessions* 5.10 (trans. R. S. Pine-Coffin [Harmondsworth and New York: Penguin, 1961], 104).

8. Ibid., 7.20 (trans. Pine-Coffin, 154).

9. Keith Ward, "God as a Principle of Cosmological Explanation," in *Quantum Cosmology and the Laws of Nature: Scientific Perspectives on Divine Action,* ed. Robert John Russell et al., 2nd ed. (Vatican City State: Vatican Observatory Foundation; Berkeley, Calif.: Center for Theology and the Natural Sciences, 1996), 258.

10. Augustine, *Confessions,* 1.2 and 10.27 (trans. Pine-Coffin, 22 and 231; translation of second passage slightly modified).

11. See John Macquarrie, *In Search of Deity: An Essay in Dialectical Theism* (New York: Crossroad, 1987), esp. 171–79.

12. Steven Weinberg, "Can Science Explain Everything? Anything?" *The New York Review of Books,* 31 May 2001, 49.

13. *The Koran* 50:16 (trans. N. J. Dawood [London and New York: Penguin, 1956], 122).

14. Rudolf Otto, *The Idea of the Holy,* 2nd ed., trans. John W. Harvey (New York: Oxford University Press, 1958).

15. Karl Schmitz-Moormann, *Theology of Creation in an Evolutionary World* (Cleveland: Pilgrim Press, 1997), 48.

16. Albert Einstein, "Religion and Science," *New York Times,* 9 November 1930, sec. 5, pp. 1–2, quoted by Max Jammer, *Einstein and Religion: Physics and Theology* (Princeton, N.J.: Princeton University Press, 1999), 80.

17. Ruth Harris, *Lourdes: Body and Spirit in the Secular Age* (New York: Viking Press, 1999), 344–45.

18. Ibid., 363.

19. Jacques Monod, *Chance and Necessity* (New York: Vintage Books, 1972), 180.

20. Jacques Monod, quoted in *Beyond Chance and Necessity,* ed. John Lewis (London: Garnstone Press, 1974), ix.

21. Karl Rahner, "Concrete Questions about Life and Psychological-Theological Answers: Interview with Karl-Heinz Weber and Hildegard Lüning, 19 March 1979," trans. Robert A. Krieg, C.S.C., in *Karl Rahner in Dialogue:*

Conversations and Interviews, 1965–1982, ed. Paul Imhof and Hubert Biallowons (New York: Crossroad, 1986), 222.

22. Pierre Teilhard de Chardin, "Some Reflections on Progress," in idem, *The Future of Man,* trans. Norman Denny (New York and Evanston: Harper and Row, 1964), 74.

23. Stephani Cook, *Second Life* (New York: Simon and Schuster, 1981), 287.

24. Schmitz-Moormann, *Theology of Creation,* 48.

25. See, e.g., Elizabeth Dodson Gray, *Green Paradise Lost: Re-mything Genesis* (Wellesley, Mass.: Roundtable Press, 1981).

26. John Chryssavgis, "Self-Image and World Image: Ecological Insights from Icons, Liturgy, and Asceticism," *Christian Spirituality Bulletin* 8, no. 1 (Spring/Summer 2001):14.

27. Ibid.

28. John Calvin, "Sermon on Deuteronomy," in *Ioannis Calvini opera quae supersunt omnia,* ed. Wilhelm Baum et al. (Brunswick: A. Schwetchke and Son, 1863–1900), 28:24.

29. Jürgen Moltmann, *God in Creation: A New Theology of Creation and the Spirit of God,* trans. Margaret Kohl (San Francisco: Harper and Row, 1985), 11.

30. Charles Cummings, *Eco-Spirituality: Toward a Reverent Life* (New York: Paulist Press, 1991), 124–25.

31. Paul Santmire, *The Travail of Nature: The Ambiguous Ecological Promise of Christian Theology* (Philadelphia: Fortress Press, 1985), 119.

Index

171